LONDON'S STRANGEST TALES

LONDON'S STRANGEST TALES

Extraordinary but true stories from over a
thousand years of London's history

TOM QUINN

PORTICO

This edition published in 2018 by
Portico, an imprint of Pavilion Books Company Ltd
43 Great Ormond Street
London
WC1N 3HZ

First published in the United Kingdom in 2016

ISBN 978-1-91162-202-4

A CIP catalogue record for this book is available from the British Library.

10 9 8 7 6 5 4 3 2

Reproduction by Colourdepth UK
Printed and bound by Imak Offset, Turkey

This book can be ordered direct from the publisher at www.pavilionbooks.com

D.A.Q. 1958–81

Thanks to Charlotte Wadham for musical interludes and to Katy, James, Alex
and Joseph for tall tales too numerous to mention. Thanks also to Katie Hewett
for skilled use of the editor's blue pencil.
The publisher would like to thank Mark Conroy for his work on the book.

CONTENTS

INTRODUCTION

Like all ancient cities, London is an extraordinarily rich source of strange tales. From stories of one-legged escalator testers and unsolved murders to flying rivers, moving churches and human lavatories.

Then there are the tales of extraordinary London characters, oddballs and inventors, mavericks and madmen – like Stanley Green, who spent his life campaigning against peanut eating, or Walter Rothschild, who taught two zebras to pull his carriage down The Mall. And away from people and places, there are the ancient rules and systems of governance that have survived the centuries to baffle historians and create numerous bizarre anomalies – dusty traditions, archaic practices and ceremonies are kept on despite, on the face of it, no longer being necessary.

Bags of nails are still paid for long-vanished plots of land, medieval legacies are still honoured each year and the pursuivants at the College of Arms still initiate prosecutions against those who infringe the rules governing the use of gules, azure and archant.

London's wealth of bizarre tales can be attributed to the city's love of the old ways, which is why much that is odd and ancient in London's social and business life survives. In the City proper, for example, an ancient ordinance defines a road as a highway without houses – which is why, to this day, no thoroughfare in the city may be called a road; it's either a street or an alley. Even big multinational corporations haven't been able to change that.

Many of London's strangest and quirkiest tales are well known to scholars but have been unavailable to the general public until now.

This book is the result of several years spent digging in obscure and dusty archives and in the libraries of organisations whose continued existence in the modern world is itself astonishing, but the labour has been worth it, for whatever your interest, whether political, social, architectural or historical, you will find *London's Strangest Tales* a mighty feast of the mad, bad, dotty, eccentric and – at times – quite unbelievable.

Tom Quinn

WHY PART OF SCOTLAND IS IN LONDON

950

Scotland Yard is famous throughout the world but few people wonder why a police station in central London should have this name. Why Scotland? The answer takes us into one of those curious and inexplicable areas of long forgotten history.

From the late tenth century until the Act of Union of 1707, which brought Scotland and England together under one Crown, Scotland was an entirely separate country with its own tradition, rules and statutes – even today Scottish law differs markedly from English law in many respects.

During the period of independence Scotland, like most foreign countries, had a London embassy and the name Great Scotland Yard is the last echo of an independent Scotland's presence in London.

Originally three streets covered this area – Little Scotland Yard and Middle Scotland Yard have long gone – but bizarrely the rules that apply to foreign embassies today still, in theory, apply to this small area of London. All embassies are in practice foreign territory – the police cannot enter a foreign embassy unless invited to do so and their jurisdiction doesn't include the territory of a foreign embassy.

After the Act of Union no one remembered to abolish the 'foreign' status of Great Scotland Yard, which means that even today the little street running off Whitehall near Trafalgar Square is actually Scottish territory.

PUT OUT YOUR FIRE

1066

Many delightful traditions linger in London long after their practical usefulness has gone. The beadle who watches Burlington Arcade, for example, forbids running, umbrellas and whistling despite the fact that these are no longer evidence of a lack of gentility. Until recently in parliament an MP under certain circumstances may only interrupt a debate if he first dons a top hat. Ravens are still kept at the Tower of London for fear that if they depart the monarchy will fall.

But perhaps the oddest and longest lasting tradition is the curfew bell still rung each evening in South Square in Gray's Inn, a centre of the legal profession since 1370.

The curfew bell rung here would have been only one of dozens rung all over medieval London, for the word curfew comes from the Norman French *couvre le feu* – meaning put out your fire – and it was rung not to tell citizens that they must not leave their houses but rather to tell them (since it was bedtime) that they should make sure they had extinguished all their fires and candles. The fear – to be realised in the terrible fire of 1666 – was that without a reminder someone might forget a candle or fire and the result would be that the thousands of dry timber and thatch buildings would ignite.

Originally, apart from the bells rung here at Gray's Inn, all London churches rang the curfew – it was on the order of William the Conqueror (1028–87) – and as late as the beginning of the Second World War a dozen or more city churches still rang the curfew. Today that 1,000-year tradition is still held in two places – Gray's Inn, as we have seen, and the Tower of London.

THE BISHOP OF WINCHESTER'S GEESE

1171

To those of a religious cast of mind it may come as a shock to discover that for centuries the Christian church made a very good living from prostitution. As it happens the Church was also one of the world's most important and vicious slave owners.

But the church in London was particularly keen to make money from prostitutes since it was so easy – in fact the prostitutes of Southwark were known as the Bishop of Winchester's geese. With magnificent hypocrisy the Bishop of Winchester was able to collect rents from the numerous brothels he owned but then when a prostitute died in the diocese the church refused to allow her to be buried in consecrated ground.

A sad little reminder of this grim and astonishing history can still be glimpsed down a quiet street in Southwark even today. Red Cross Way runs parallel to Borough High Street and if you follow it almost as far as the junction with Union Street you come to a rusty iron gate and behind it a plot of land.

This is the remnant of Cross Bones Graveyard where the Bishop of Winchester's geese were buried when they could no longer earn money for the church.

A royal ordinance of 1171 allowed the Bishop of Winchester to license the brothels, or stews as they were known, and to collect the income. The Bishop's jurisdiction covered what was known as the Liberty of the Clink – the reference is to the Clink Prison, part of which can still be seen in the Anchor Inn, a few hundred yards along the riverbank west from Southwark Cathedral.

In 1833 a history of the area mentions the 'unconsecrated burial ground known as the Cross Bones at the corner of Redcross Street, formerly called the Single Woman's burial ground ...'. The writer is clearly echoing the words of a much earlier author, John Stow (1525–1605), whose great *Survey of London* was published in 1598.

Stow refers to Cross Bones and 'these single women who were forbidden the rites of the church, so long as they continued that sinful life, and were excluded from Christian burial, if they were not reconciled before their death. And therefore there was a plot of ground called the Single Woman's Churchyard, appointed for them far from the parish church.'

The brothels, drinking houses, bear-pits and cock-pits of Southwark survived until the death of Charles I on the scaffold in 1649 and the arrival of Oliver Cromwell and a Puritan-dominated government, but when the prostitutes – or most of them – departed, the poor arrived in their droves and by the middle of the nineteenth century this was one of the foulest and most overcrowded parts of London. It was also dangerous – so dangerous in fact that even the police were reluctant to stray too far into its warren of filthy, rat-infested streets and alleys. Cross Bones Graveyard continued to be used until 1853 when the bodies were being buried so close to the surface that decaying hands and feet were often seen sticking through the soil. The government insisted it be closed.

But if proof were needed that the patch of ground that remains really was a burial ground for the Southwark geese, an excavation in 1990 discovered almost 150 skeletons, mostly women and one with the clear marks of syphilis.

With typical greed the authorities have tried again and

again to build on the remaining plot of land but fierce local opposition has ensured that, at least for the time being, the old graveyard of Southwark's geese remains as a monument to a long-vanished part of London's medieval history.

SQUABBLING CHURCHMEN

1176

Even the earliest gospels were written almost a century after the death of Jesus, so it is no wonder that they are full of inconsistencies – some make no mention of Christ's supposed divinity, some make no mention of his brothers and sisters (the Catholic Church couldn't bear the idea that Mary had children other than Jesus) so it is perhaps not surprising that as the centuries passed the Christian religion had far more to do with the church and the authority of its members than with Christ himself. Endless squabbles about what Christ really meant and of what he might have approved or disapproved led eventually to schism and the passionate desire of Christians of every persuasion to burn each other to death.

One of the most hilarious of these ancient squabbles took place in Westminster Abbey in the second half of the twelfth century. Until this time priests had been perfectly entitled to marry and it was an entirely arbitrary decision to forbid something that had been acceptable for more than a thousand years. Other disputes centred on the differences between the ancient rites of the church inherited through the Irish tradition and the growing authority of Rome, whose traditions were very different in many particulars.

The Archbishop of York (Irish tradition) was convinced that he was the senior English cleric, but this infuriated the Archbishop of Canterbury (Rome) who refused to accept that anyone should even think of taking precedence over him.

Things came to a head when a papal legate visited England in 1176. The legate decided to sort out the question once and for all by convening a synod at Westminster Abbey.

It took the Archbishop of York much longer to get to London for the synod than his co-religionist from Canterbury. When he arrived and entered Westminster Abbey he found the Archbishop of Canterbury already seated in the position of precedence on the right of the papal legate. He was so furious that he marched up to the papal legate and sat on his lap, to the astonishment of the other bishops!

According to contemporary reports a fight ensued with ecclesiastical supporters of Canterbury attacking supporters of York – even the papal legate could do nothing to quell the riot. But the legate was a clever man who quickly saw a way through the problem – following debate at the synod (after everyone had calmed down) he determined that the Archbishop of York should be Primate of England and the Archbishop of Canterbury should be Primate of All England. This master-piece of fudging has lasted down to the present day.

HUMAN LAVATORY

1190

As successive British governments have closed Britain's once great wealth of public lavatories – London's loos, until the 1950s, were famous the world over – so has the public been forced to dash in and out of restaurants and pubs where they have no intention either of eating or drinking.

The reason London's magnificent Victorian public loos were built in the first place was simply that governments of the time saw them as essential to the well-being of Londoners. Parliamentarians who knew their history far better than today's legislators no doubt remembered that right through the Middle Ages and well into the seventeenth century one of London's biggest problems was the lack of public loos.

In their houses people simply used a bucket or pot and then threw the contents into the gutter or the Thames. There is much evidence to suggest that many householders – this was certainly true in aristocratic households – simply relieved themselves in the corner of any room they happened to be in.

Out in the streets people relieved themselves wherever they liked, but the more delicate-minded and, of course, women found this unacceptable – the solution was provided by human loos.

These were men and women who wore voluminous black capes and carried a bucket. When you needed the loo you looked for the nearest man or woman with a cape and bucket and gave them a farthing. You then sat on the bucket while they stood above you still wearing the cape but also surrounding you with it.

The name of only one human lavatory has come down to us – the court rolls reveal that in 1190 one Thomas Butcher of Cheapside was fined 'and admonished' for overcharging his clients.

THE RIGHT TO BE
HANGED BY SILK

1237

The first freedom of the city of London was given in 1237. In late medieval England being granted the freedom of the city was not a courtesy title nor a simple invitation to wander the city at will. Instead it had enormous practical importance. Once granted it meant the recipient was freed from his duty to his feudal lord – he was a free agent and under the terms of the granting of freedom it meant he could own land and earn money in his own right. He was also protected from feudal duties – the duty of military service for example – because he had rights under the charter of the city. These rights were so important that they could occasionally conflict with the rights of the monarch.

The city authorities were careful, however, to ensure that so far as possible the monarch was central to the granting of freedom. The freedom of the city is still granted today and those accepting it have to swear the following oath:

I do solemnly swear that I will be good and true to our Sovereign; that I will be obedient to the Mayor of this City; that I will maintain the Franchises and Customs thereof, and will keep this City harmless, in that which is in me; that I will also keep the Queen's Peace in my own person; that I will know no Gatherings nor Conspiracies made against the Queen's Peace, but I will warn the Mayor thereof, or hinder it to my power; and that all these points and articles I will well and truly keep, according to the Laws and Customs of this City, to my power.

Once he agreed to this the freeman was given a parchment and a wooden casket in which to keep it – in medieval times it is believed that many freemen refused to leave their houses without taking with them – rather like a modern passport – the parchment that confirmed their status as freemen.

Some of the rights granted to freemen are bizarre by any standards – although today they are merely symbolic, a freeman is entitled to herd sheep over London Bridge, he may walk about the city with a drawn sword, can insist on being married in St Paul's Cathedral, is permitted to be drunk and disorderly without fear of arrest and best of all if he is sentenced to hang, he has the right to insist that the executioner uses a silken rope!

A PIECE OF
CAMBRIDGESHIRE
IN LONDON

1290

The rationalisation of London's boundaries and the counties that border the capital destroyed some wonderfully comic anomalies. Middlesex, for example, was once split in two – Epping Forest, which is now in Essex, was once in the eastern portion of Middlesex while Uxbridge far away to the west was in the western portion. Between the two parts of Middlesex was a substantial stretch of Hertfordshire!

Most but not all of these anomalies have vanished. One of the most interesting and unusual that remains is centred on Ely Place just off High Holborn and a little above the course of the now covered River Fleet.

It is one of the few places that still embodies the ancient rivalry between the Lord Mayor and the monarch, for within the city boundaries the mayor is in charge and successive monarchs have had to accept this. They, in turn, have made sure that the mayor's jurisdiction is kept rigidly within the bounds of the old city limits. Traditionally the monarch has to ask permission to enter the city, which used to happen every year at a special ceremony at Temple Bar in the Strand.

Ely Place is within the city boundary but is owned by the Crown. Because of this, it is exempt from the authority of the Lord Mayor and is still – even today – a private road with its own gates and a beadle. Even the police may enter this street only with the permission of the beadle.

Ely Place has a long and unusual history. Successive Bishops of Ely had their London palace here from 1290 until 1772 when, neglected and almost ruinous, it was demolished. The church of St Ethelreda, which is still here, was completed in about 1291 and is the oldest Roman Catholic pre-Reformation church in London – although church is a rather grand term for what was and is a small private chapel.

The Palace had many famous residents over the years – John of Gaunt lived here from 1381 until his death in 1391 and Henry VIII was an occasional visitor, as was his daughter Elizabeth I.

There is a delightful story of Elizabeth insisting that the Bishop of Ely should rent some part of the palace to her courtier Sir Christopher Hatton, whose name is commemorated in the diamond merchant district of nearby Hatton Garden. The bishop was told he could charge Hatton 'ten pounds a year, ten loads of hay and a rose picked at midsummer'.

Until about 1920 a policeman had to be dispatched from Ely, 100 miles (161km) away in Cambridgeshire, to police the street because officially this is part of Cambridgeshire!

The houses which now surround St Ethelreda's were built at the end of the eighteenth century and until recently Britain's only diamond cleaver carried on his business in one of them.

In his play, Richard III, Shakespeare mentions the wonderful strawberries that once grew here in the gardens of the old Palace.

HOW THE WOMEN
BEAT THE LAWYERS

1314

Lawyers have always been hated. Even when we need them most we think of them as arrogant parasites whose trade union – the Law Society – regulates their affairs in such a way as to ensure their fees are always exorbitant. In surveys lawyers are always voted among the worst professionals, only a little behind journalists.

Perhaps one reason for this is the curious history of the legal profession in Britain. The lawyers' history is intimately tied up with their presence in the Inns of Court.

Lawyers arrived on the site they still occupy between Fleet Street and the river in the early fourteenth century when they took a lease on land formerly owned by the Knights Templar, whose order had been proscribed by the Pope in 1314.

The lawyers took the lease on the site because Henry III, who had established a law school at Oxford, did not want a rival lawyers' college in the City of London. The lawyers didn't like this so they retaliated by establishing their Inns (the first buildings were designed as a hotel for lawyers – hence the name 'inn') outside the City boundaries. In other words, in typical lawyer fashion, they avoided legislation they didn't like by exploiting a loophole! But there was a price to pay for what turned into a centuries long battle between the lawyers and the City authorities.

On three occasions in the late medieval period the Mayor

of London attempted to enter the Inns of Court; each time the lawyers slammed the doors in his face and threatened to fight him and his men if they attempted to break down the gates. The Mayor appealed to the King who was forced to seek legal advice – the result of course was a foregone conclusion and the lawyers advised in their own favour.

The City didn't forget the slight and when a major fire broke out in the Temple they refused to help put it out. Legend has it that the lawyers raided their vast cellars and found enough beer to put the flames out unaided!

Just before the Great War in 1913 the lawyers' sense that they were outside the law was tested when the City coroner tried to enter the Temple to register a death. The gates were slammed in his face and nothing could be done. Today, according to legend, the lawyers refuse to pay council tax or business rates in the normal way – they insist on deciding themselves just how much they will or will not pay.

It took several centuries for the lawyers to persuade the Crown to sell them the land they had leased since the fourteenth century. James I finally gave in but he did so reluctantly – so much so that the lawyers were fearful he would change his mind. To prevent any going back they buried their freehold agreement beneath the altar in the Temple church where it remained until early in the twentieth century.

The person with ultimate control of the lawyers here on the banks of the Thames is the Master of the Temple. In the past, masters thought of themselves as easily the equal if not the superior of the Mayor of London and they took their duties very seriously. One of these duties was looking after the moral welfare of the junior members of the inn. A Victorian master decided that too many young lawyers were bringing women into the inn so he decided to put a stop to it by issuing a directive that all women coming into the Temple must in future sign their names in a ledger together with the name of the lawyer they were visiting.

Imagine the poor master's horror when he discovered a few days after the new rule was in place that hundreds of young women had signed themselves in and put his name down as the lawyer they were visiting!

PLANNING FOR CENTURIES AHEAD

1399

When a new building goes up the builders and planners never think of how that building may (or may not) survive into the near future let alone the more distant future, but in the past buildings were put up that were meant – at least when they were built – to last forever. A case in point is Westminster Hall, whose builders came up with an extraordinary idea to ensure that it would last for generations.

The lower parts of the walls of Westminster Hall, which seem now to the casual observer to be part of the Georgian Palace of Westminster, are actually unchanged since this huge building was begun shortly after the Norman Conquest of 1066. The earliest work is dated to the end of the eleventh century and what we see today is the building that was finally completed in 1399. The hall has one of the greatest architectural treasures of the late Middle Ages – the vast, intricate and magnificent hammer-beam roof. Like any ancient building Westminster Hall has needed to be repaired now and then: parts of the walls were rebuilt or repaired along with the windows in earlier centuries; the roof too has been renewed here and there as the ancient timbers have decayed, and a section had to be replaced after a bomb caused some damage in the 1980s.

The last major period of restoration was in 1913 when several major timbers had to be renewed. But this presented the board of works with a major headache. England's oak woods had long ago been felled and officials simply could not find a plantation with oaks big enough to provide the right sort of timber. Oak trees there were but they were perhaps 200 or 300 years old and therefore simply not big enough. What was to be done?

Then someone had the bright idea of checking where the original timbers had come from. It was discovered that at the end of the fourteenth century they had been brought to Westminster from an estate near Wadhurst in East Sussex. The estate had been owned at that time – nearly 500 years earlier – by the Courthorpe family. In 1913 there was a descendant of the original Courthorpe family in Parliament – he was MP for Rye, the beautiful Cinque Port on the south coast. When he was approached Sir George Courthorpe astonished officials with the following story. He explained that when the original trees had been cut and sold to the king in the fourteenth century, Courthorpe's ancestors had thought that the time would come when the timbers needed repair or renewal so they planted a new stand of oak trees specifically for the purpose.

Those trees were now – in 1913 – ready and they were duly cut and used to repair the great roof of Westminster Hall.

GROPECUNT LANE
1450

We tend to think of the modern world as a place where anything goes – we take a very liberal view of swearing and sexual morality and we imagine that all other ages before ours were characterised by strict prudish morality, a morality typified by the Victorians who are popularly supposed to have covered the legs of their tables as the very idea of any sort of leg on display was shocking to them.

The Victorians may well have been excessively prudish, worthy and hypocritical, but it is completely wrong to imagine that all other earlier epochs were similar – there have been many periods in the past that have taken a far more liberal view of life in general than the modern age.

During Charles II's reign, for example, Nell Gwynn (1651–87) was adored by Londoners who loathed the king's French wife and this despite the fact that Nell was always referred to as the king's whore. Whore in the seventeenth century seems to have lacked at least some of the harsher overtones that it now has.

Charles II himself cared little for traditional morality – he allowed plays to be written and performed that made the pursuit of pleasure, particularly sexual pleasure, the centre and mainspring of life. Puritan London was scandalised but there was little the religious could do as the plays had the king's sanction.

In medieval London too, sex was far more acceptable in a public context than it is now – anyone who looks at a map of London produced before 1450 will see several street names that are so extraordinary by our standards that they simply would not be allowed today.

Addle Street appears on these earlier maps, for example, and to a medieval Londoner Addle Street mean 'filthy spot'. Or take Fetter Lane, which still exists – in 1450 it meant the street of the dirty beggars.

Other names were dropped after the Reformation as the influence of killjoy Protestants came to dominate public life. Public holidays on saint's days were largely abandoned and many London street names were changed. Shiteburn Lane near Canon Street – so named because of the number of cesspits to be found here – was changed to the far more genteel sounding Sherborne Lane, a name it retains to this day.

But the most extraordinary street of all, that vanished with the arrival of the Reformation and the serious sensibility that seems to have accompanied it, was a small lane that ran north from Cheapside. It was called Gropecunt Lane for the simple reason that it was a famous haunt of prostitutes.

WHY WE SAY SIXES
AND SEVENS

1490

Only London would retain something as dotty as a company of tailors who have had absolutely nothing to do with making clothes for more than 300 years.

But like most London guilds, the Merchant Taylors have long since lost all connection with their original calling. Most guilds exist – again like the tailors – merely to administer ancient and sometimes more recent charitable bequests.

The Merchant Taylors – now rather sadly run by grey men in suits – still has some 300 members and they administer a number of charities including alms houses in south London, a school in north London and a number of churches. But they have enjoyed – or suffered – a turbulent and fascinating history. Perhaps most interestingly, the Merchant Taylors are also responsible for that curious phrase where one describes a state of chaos or indecision as 'being at sixes and sevens'.

To find out how this odd phrase came into the language we need to take a brief look at the early history of the guild.

The Merchant Taylors, who were later joined by the Linen Armourers, originally made clothes – but most particularly a medieval jacket called a gambeson. This was a thick padded jacket – padded because it was worn in battle either under armour, by the nobility, or on its own by the common soldiers. As the gambeson fell out of use with the introduction of firearms and abandonment of swords and pikes, the Merchant Taylors moved on to make tents for the army until sometime in the seventeenth century even this became a pointless exercise.

The company received its charter as early as 1327 and is, as a result, considered one of the 12 great livery companies. These tend to be the most ancient companies and they include the mercers, drapers, fishmongers and goldsmiths. They were livery companies because members of particular guilds wore distinctive clothes (or livery).

In its Royal Charter of 1503, the guild is given its full name – 'The Gild of Merchant Taylors of the Fraternity of St. John Baptist in the City of London.'

Early in their history the guilds were jealous of their status and fought for their place in the order of precedence during any progress of the Lord Mayor across London.

After endless arguments with the Guild of Skinners about who should take sixth place in the order of precedence and who seventh, the Lord Mayor of London issued an order in the late fifteenth century to the effect that the Skinners and Merchant Taylors would alternate in precedence: in odd-numbered years the Merchant Taylors would be sixth in order; in even years the Skinners would take the sixth place and the Merchant Taylors would be seventh. Hence the phrase – to be at sixes and sevens.

The alternating precedence continues to this day.

THE HOUSE THAT SHAKESPEARE KNEW?

1502

Few domestic houses in central London can lay claim to as many strange tales as a tall, narrow house that stands on the south bank of the Thames looking towards St Paul's Cathedral and close to the site of Shakespeare's original Globe Theatre.

The fact that the house is still standing is a remarkable tale in itself for this elegant narrow building – once part of a terrace – is the last remaining of the many Bankside houses that once lined the river here. On the wall next to the front door of number 49 is a plaque that bears the name of a very famous Englishman, as well as that of a Spanish princess who inadvertently changed the course of British history. The plaque claims: 'Here lived Sir Christopher Wren during the building of St Paul's Cathedral. Here also, in 1502, Catherine Infanta of Castile and Aragon, afterwards first queen of Henry VIII, took shelter on her first landing in London.'

However, as with many London tales, all is not quite as it seems. While the information written on the plaque was taken at face value for many years, subsequent research has uncovered quite a different story.

Sir Christopher Wren certainly stayed close to St Paul's during its construction in the early eighteenth century, but in a house a few doors down that no longer exists. And although it was built over the foundations of an original

Elizabethan building, number 49 was not built until 1710 –
the year St Paul's Cathedral was completed.

Research also suggests that it was highly unlikely that
the future queen of England would have stayed in a
modest building alongside the River Thames in a less than
salubrious area.

Running down one side of the house – sadly now closed
to the public – is one of London's narrowest thoroughfares
– Cardinal Cap Alley. In its early years this was a poor
and dangerous part of London – apart from the theatres
(banished to the south side of the river by the more
religious-minded members of the government who thought
plays immoral) the area was also famous for its bear-baiting
and cock-fighting pits, as well as for the sheer number of
its brothels. The murder rate here was probably twice that
of the city across the water and there are vague references
to respectable citizens simply disappearing in the vicinity of
Cardinals Wharf – at least one twentieth-century owner of
the house said he would never excavate below the house for
fear of what he might find!

ROBBING PETER TO PAY PAUL

1540

Few people today realise that Westminster Abbey is not the name of the great abbey church that stands at Westminster. The official name of the abbey is the Collegiate Church of St Peter at Westminster and it is from this name that the phrase 'robbing Peter to pay Paul' comes. Today the phrase simply means taking money from, as it were, the left hand and giving it to the right or to pay one person at the pointless expense of another person.

The origins of the phrase lie in those decades after the Reformation of the mid-1500s that ended Britain's 1,000-year monastic tradition. After Henry VIII's death his son Edward VI (1537–53) continued the work of giving monastic lands and money to his favourites. The new parish churches also competed for endowments and Westminster Abbey (St Peter's) petitioned the king endlessly for funding. So much so that he decided to punish the abbey by taking away the revenues St Peter's had long enjoyed from the Manor of Paddington and giving them to St Paul's, which had always been known as London's cathedral. Thus the Royal church lost out to the London cathedral – and the phrase 'robbing Peter to pay Paul' came into the language.

VANISHED DUNGEONS REAPPEAR

1555

Many villages and country towns in England still have their ancient lock-ups – these are small, usually single-roomed buildings, often near the market square or by the side of a back street, that were once used to house those arrested before they could be taken to court and dealt with by local magistrates. They were also used simply to get someone unruly off the streets for the night – a drunk perhaps – and having sobered up the miscreant would then be released the next day.

The City of London had similar though usually larger lock-ups until fairly recent times – but in the City they were and are called compters. The original compter buildings have, like so much of London's history, been swept away but here and there the underground cells of former compters do survive.

Casual passers-by would be astonished to discover that what may well have once been the dungeons of the formerly infamous Wood Street Compter – situated in Mitre Court in the City – can still be seen complete with their chains and fetters. Mitre Court gets its name from the celebrated Mitre Tavern that once stood here – it is mentioned by countless writers and features in Ben Jonson's (1572–1637) play *Bartholomew Fair*.

The compter once housed some 70 prisoners. It was built in 1555 and was under the control of the sheriffs of London.

It seems to have been used as a lock-up but also, curiously, as a debtor's prison and even to house the overflow of prisoners when nearby Newgate was full.

For centuries all trace of it was assumed to have vanished but early in the twentieth century the former dungeons were rediscovered. One wonders how many other parts of ancient London buildings remain underground and awaiting rediscovery.

The compter was unusual in reflecting precisely the social conditions outside the prison: it had three sections – the best section, the master's side as it was known, was for the wealthy and aristocratic; the knight's side was for those of some means, however small; and the hole was for the common people. The surviving cellars – now part of a nearby wine merchant – may well have been part of the hole, the most feared part of the prison and in which incarceration meant you were very likely to die from typhoid, cholera or some other waterborne disease.

THE QUEEN'S BOSOM ON SHOW

1597

Detailed descriptions of the London scene before 1600 are
relatively rare. Those that exist only occasionally satisfy the
modern desire for detail – published descriptions mention
noble buildings, grand thoroughfares and monumental
edifices, but they rarely describe what it was actually like to
walk along the Strand, through the mud and the puddles,
when the City wall still existed and the Strand was effectively
a suburb where the rich had their riverside palaces.

But if physical, detailed descriptions are lacking we are
lucky enough to have a number of wonderful descriptions
of meetings with the great and the good.

When the French ambassador Andre Hurhault-Sieur de
Maisse met Queen Elizabeth I for the first time in 1597 she
had been on the throne for almost 40 years, a remarkably
long reign in an age of regular outbreaks of the plague and
general medical ignorance.

It had taken more than a year for the French ambassador
to finally fix a date for the meeting and his sense that this
was a momentous and long-awaited event comes through
in the detailed report he wrote afterwards.

De Maisse was led along a dark corridor to the audience
chamber where the Queen sat on a low chair. Others in the
room gathered in small groups at some distance from her.
The ambassador made a low bow at the door and the Queen
rose and came over to him. De Maisse takes up the story:

I kissed the fringe of her robe and she embraced me with both arms. She smiled at me, and began to apologise for not receiving me sooner. She said that the day before she had been very ill.

She was dressed in silver cloth, her dress with slashed sleeves lined with red taffeta. On her head she wore a garland and beneath it a great reddish-coloured wig, with a great number of spangles of gold and silver, and hanging down over her forehead some pearls, but of no great worth.

By this time the Queen was in her sixties. Her cheeks were sunken and her teeth were yellow and broken with many missing from her habit of continually eating sweets – in fact so many teeth were missing that it was difficult at times for De Maisse to understand what she was saying. De Maisse noticed all this and was therefore doubly astonished to discover that she was actually half naked! He explains with evident astonishment that the Queen's dress was completely open down the front and that her breasts – which she continually handled and moved about – were completely open to view.

He says: 'Her bosom is somewhat wrinkled as well as one can see for the collar that she wears round her neck, but lower down her flesh is exceeding white and delicate, so far as one could see.'

The only explanation one can find at this distance in time is that the Queen, who could never be criticised or contradicted, really believed the stories her poets and painters told her – that she was the eternally youthful Virgin Queen. The creature she read about in the verses presented to her was daily confirmed by her courtiers' behaviour and she clearly believed it all – either that or by this time she was simply losing her marbles!

Queen Elizabeth I, who could never be criticised or contradicted,
really believed the stories her poets and painters told her – that she was
the eternally youthful Virgin Queen.

LONDON'S ONLY
MAN-MADE RIVER
1606

With the growth of international trade, the founding of the South Sea Company and other trading groups, seventeenth-century London had a huge and ever increasing problem: how to get enough clean water for the population; and not just the human population – thousands of horses on which the city relied for transport had also to be watered regularly. The Thames was dirty and the water polluted, which caused regular epidemics.

One of the very earliest attempts to find a solution to the water problems can still be seen in north London.

Along the backs of the houses in one or two streets in Canonbury, the most prestigious and expensive part of Islington, runs a narrow watercourse. To the casual observer it looks like an old canal, but a closer inspection reveals something rather odd – this river is far too narrow to be a canal, but it isn't a river or a stream either. It is in fact one of the last remnants of one of the earliest attempts to bring fresh water to London.

The New River Company started life in 1606 when Acts of Parliament were passed to enable a channel to be dug to bring fresh water to central London from Amwell in Hertfordshire. Londoners were aware that it was unhealthy to throw all their rubbish and sewage into the same river from which they obtained their drinking water (i.e. the Thames) but the practical difficulties of finding a supply other than the Thames had always seemed insurmountable. The New River Company refused to accept defeat. The head of the company – Hugh Myddleton (1560–1631) – began the enormous task of digging the channel, which was to become the New River. It was to be 10ft (3m) wide by 4ft (1.2m) deep. Total length was a little less than 40 miles (64.3km). All the work had to be done by hand and much of it was carried out in the face of fierce opposition from landowners along the route. Halfway through the work Myddleton ran out of money and had to be rescued by King James, who offered financial assistance in return for a share of future profits.

By 1613 the route had been completed and water ran into four newly built reservoirs at Clerkenwell. From here it ran to the city through wooden pipes – pipes which are still occasionally uncovered today during roadworks and re-building. Though the system leaked badly it was to provide water for many in the city for more than 200 years.

The New River was adapted over the centuries and its flow was increased by additions from various newly dug wells and from the River Lea, but in essence it remained unchanged until 1904 when the New River Company was amalgamated with the Metropolitan Water Board. When the Second World War ended a decision was made to stop using water from the remaining reservoirs at Clerkenwell and though the flow continues to this day it now ends at Stoke Newington. However, a few stretches of the channel much closer to central London have survived, including those quiet backwaters running through Canonbury.

JOHN DONNE, UNDONE

1631

The author of some of the greatest short poems of the seventeenth century, John Donne (1573–1631), is buried in St Paul's Cathedral where he was dean for a number of years. Donne is the author of many famous lines that have passed into the language – 'no man is an island', for example, and 'ask not for whom the bell tolls; it tolls for thee' – but in addition to writing verse he was a busy public man who sat as an MP in Elizabeth I's last parliament and worked for some time as a lawyer before taking holy orders.

By the time he entered the church he was already in middle age and probably a little embarrassed about his earlier versifying days. His piety certainly seems to have increased and towards the end of his life he commissioned a portrait on which to base his own monument, which was to be a life-sized marble statue showing the poet in his shroud and peeping gloomily out from the folds of its hood. According to his contemporary and biographer, Izaak Walton, he rose from his deathbed to pose for the artist, stripped naked and holding his own funeral shroud around him.

When he died on 31 March 1631, a statue was created by sculptor Nicholas Stone and placed in St Paul's within 18 months of his death.

Nearly half a century later, of course, St Paul's burned down destroying pretty much everything within the church with one exception – John Donne's monument. Visitors today can still see the smoke-blackened lower parts of the marble – the only visible evidence of the Great Fire that consumed so much of London in 1666 – but Donne peeps out from his hood unperturbed. The words Donne wrote in prison following an early, clandestine marriage were perhaps never more pertinent, 'John Donne … Undone.'

A CHURCH THE WRONG
WAY ROUND

1631

St Paul's Covent Garden is one of London's quirkiest churches. It was built as part of London's first planned square in 1631. Its architect – he was also the architect of the square and all the houses in it – was the great Inigo Jones, who had studied the work of Palladio in Italy and longed to produce something similar in London.

The idea of a square surrounded on three sides by collonaded walks was met with derision by Londoners but the Duke of Bedford, one of London's richest men and a great enthusiast for all things Italian, pressed ahead anyway.

The houses were built and were immediately popular with London's fashionable elite despite those early misgivings. But the church that Jones was asked to build at the west end of the square is bizarre because it is built the wrong way round.

Problems began when the Duke of Bedford, who seems to have been keen for the houses to be beautifully built, told Jones that he really didn't care much for the idea of a church at all and that therefore it was to be built as cheaply as possible – 'I want it little better than a barn,' he is reputed to have said – but Jones, being proud of his work, decided that he would build magnificently anyway: 'I will build the handsomest barn in England,' he claimed.

The planned design involved having a main entrance into the square – in other words at the east end of the church

– but when Archbishop Laud got wind of the plan he was furious and, despite the fact that the church was almost complete, he ordered that the east end of the church be blocked up and that the entrance should be rebuilt at the west end where it remains to this day. The heavy portico at the east end, reminds us that this should originally have been the grand entrance.

It is ironic that the building on which least care was lavished, officially at least, is the only one to survive from Inigo Jones's time. During the years of Covent Garden's fame – which lasted until the end of the seventeenth century – the houses were proudly kept, but as the fashionable moved out in the eighteenth century, the square became famous for its brothels and gin shops.

This was caused partly by the growth of the vegetable market, which had started in the middle decades of the seventeenth century but had grown enormously a century later. With late-night revellers from the theatres, gin palaces and coffee houses open all night to service the market porters, the area lost its reputation as a genteel district and became the debauched squalid place depicted in Hogarth's 'Morning' from the series *Four Times of the Day*.

Inigo Jones's plan for a piazza made the word fashionable for decades and hundreds of London girls were christened 'Piazza' in the years up to 1650.

POET BURIED
STANDING UP

1637

Westminster Abbey has long been the last resting place of the great, the good, the brave – and the poetically inclined. Among the more interesting epitaphs is T.S. Eliot's (1888–1965) splendidly enigmatic:

> The communication of the dead
> Is tongued with fire beyond the language of the living.

The lines come from Eliot's own great poem *Four Quartets*. But the strangest monument in the abbey seems remarkably unassuming on the face of it – a small stone, moved from the floor of the abbey to a wall in the last century to protect it from wear and tear, reads simply: 'O rare Johnson'. The lines (including the mis-spelled surname – it should be Jonson!) were written by the now forgotten poet Jack Young and they refer to the great Elizabethan and Jacobean playwright Ben Jonson (1572–1637), who is buried in the abbey in a most unusual way. Jonson, the son of a bricklayer, was extraordinarily lucky as a child to come to the attention of the antiquary William Camden, then a master at Westminster School. Camden paid for Jonson's schooling and in robbing us of a master bricklayer he gave us instead a master playwright. Jonson's comic masterpieces *Every Man in his Humour*, *Bartholomew Fair*, *Volpone* and *The Alchemist* are unlikely ever to be forgotten and they were hugely popular in his lifetime, but despite his success Jonson was not a good businessman like his contemporary William Shakespeare.

Where Shakespeare invested his money in land and property, Jonson seems to have spent his on wild living – in a drunken brawl he killed a fellow poet and only escaped hanging because he was able to plead benefit of clergy. In Elizabethan England, bizarrely, a man who had committed murder but could read Latin was not executed. Instead his thumb would be branded – as was Jonson's – with the letter M.

Towards the end of his life, and still living in poverty, Jonson is supposed to have discussed his funeral arrangements with the Dean of Westminster. 'I am too poor to be buried in the abbey,' he is reported to have said, 'And no one will lay out my funeral charges. Six feet long by two feet wide is too much for me. Two feet by two feet will do.'

The dean is said to have immediately promised Jonson he could have his tiny area in what was to become known as Poets' Corner, clearly thinking that Jonson intended only to have a small memorial attached to the spot. In fact Jonson was properly buried in the abbey when the time came – he did it by arranging to have himself buried standing bolt upright in his grave where he remains to this day. It was his final joke.

In the 1840s work on the floor of the abbey disturbed the grave and Jonson's leg bones were found standing upright; his skull was intact too and apparently still with red hair attached to it!

Other graves in Westminster Abbey have strange stories attached to them – the poet Byron (1788–1824) was not commemorated here until 1967 because of his disreputable lifestyle (despite the fame of his poetry) and even Shakespeare had to wait until 1740 for a monument to be erected for him. The difficulty for the authorities when they thought of Shakespeare was reconciling themselves to the fact that despite being a commoner with only a relatively rudimentary education he became and remains the greatest writer in the English language – perhaps in any language. The same feeling of unease has fuelled numerous claims over the centuries that other more aristocratic scribblers are responsible for the plays and poems and merely used Shakespeare's name.

A SQUARE OF WONDERS

1641

There are lots of wonderfully odd things about Lincoln's Inn Fields. The name reminds us that this was, for centuries, open ground where the lawyers from the Inns of Court enjoyed walking, so much that when building began in the 1640s, a deputation from the lawyers to the builders persuaded them not to cover the whole site with new houses, but instead to leave the central area open, which is just as it remains to this day.

Other oddities about the square include Sir John Soane's (1753–1837) extraordinary house – rarely can a single, relatively small house have been so stuffed with antiquities. Special cupboards and sliding display cases of great ingenuity and complexity had to be built at great expense to house Sir John's vast collection in such a small space. The house is now open to the public.

The square was and is also home to the Royal College of Surgeons – in earlier times tumbrils travelled regularly across the square carrying the bodies of the recently executed for dissection at the college. And in the college museum is the skeleton of Jonathan Wilde, the famous highwayman who was also the model for John Gay's (1685–1732) celebrated character Macheath in *The Beggar's Opera*.

The square was the scene of an encounter that typified the reasons for the seventeenth-century Londoner's love of 'pretty, witty' Nell Gwynn, Charles II's favourite mistress. Stories about Nell abound but two of the best concern her time here in Lincoln's Inn Fields. Travelling here from Covent Garden one summer day she found herself surrounded by a mob that jostled her coach. She quickly realised that the angry crowd thought she was Charles's very unpopular French mistress, Catholic Louise de Keroualle (1649–1734). With great presence of mind Nell straightaway stuck her head out the window and shouted: 'Pray good people be civil, I am the Protestant whore!'

On another occasion she sat in her house in Lincoln's Inn with her son by Charles II playing nearby. The boy was aged about five. Nell was irritated that Charles had so far done nothing for the boy but she knew that direct appeals to him would do nothing. When he arrived to see her he played with his son for a while but the boy then ran off to the other side of the room and wouldn't return. Nelly saw her chance: 'Come here, you little bastard!' she shouted. Charles was horrified. 'Why do you use that terrible name?' he asked. 'Well, you have given him no other,' she replied. Charles promptly made the boy Duke of St Albans with land and an income that his descendants enjoy to this day.

But without question the oddest aspect of Lincoln's Inn Fields is that its dimensions are precisely those of the base of the Great Pyramid at Giza!

STRANGLED HARES FOR
KIDNEY STONES

1658

In earlier centuries the idea of objective truth – in the scientific sense in which we might understand that term today – was largely absent. Medical, scientific and religious experts relied on authority: in other words if the great and the good said something was true then that was accepted for centuries without anyone ever worrying about proof.

A good example is the huge number of strange books of cures and medical preparations published over the centurics. In the late seventeenth century there seems to have been something of a flurry of medical publications emanating from London and all claiming that the cures they detailed for everything from the gout to the plague were published on the best authority – in other words they were the ideas of well-known doctors. No one seems ever to have worried about whether these various cures actually worked, which is astonishing when one reads the ingredients of the cures given for various ailments.

The following is a good example. It's a cure for kidney stones and comes from a book of medical recipes published at the Angel in Cornhill in 1658:

In the month of May distil Cow dung, then take two live Hares, and strangle them in their Blood, then take the one of them, and put it into an earthen vessel or pot, and cover it well with a mortar made of horse dung and hay, and bake it in an Oven with household bread, and let it still in an Oven two or three days, baking anew with anything, until the Hare be baked or dried to powder, then beat it well, and keep it for your use. The other Hare you must flea and take out the guts only, then distil al the rest, and keep this water: then take at the new and full of the Moon, or any other time, three mornings together as much of this powder as will lie on a sixpence, with two spoonfuls of each water, and it will break any stone in the kidneys.

How could this – and dozens of equally unlikely recipes – ever have been written down with any confidence as a genuine cure for kidney stones? Impossible though it is to believe, perhaps it really did work! More likely is that as a number of kidney-stone sufferers managed to pass the stones in their urine anyway – thus becoming cured – this vile mixture or something similar came to be given the credit for those who would have recovered unaided anyway.

WHY TEACHERS
HAVE TO BE BETTER
THAN THE KING

1660

Despite George Bernard Shaw's foolish quip – 'Those who can do, those who can't teach' – the whole future of each generation depends to a large degree on the skills or otherwise of the teaching profession. Given that undeniable fact it is astonishing that teachers are not held in higher esteem – in the past things were very different and a teacher was absolute ruler in his little kingdom, which may explain why teachers were permitted far greater liberties: children could be flogged until well within living memory and for the least mistake or misdemeanour.

The teaching profession was also a great producer of eccentrics – some would say madmen – and among the maddest was undoubtedly Dr Richard Busby (1606–95).

A prolific author of Latin texts, he was educated at Westminster School where he was later to become headmaster, a role he filled for an astonishing 58 years, and in all that time his proud boast was that not one boy had passed through the school without being personally flogged by the good and no doubt deeply religious doctor. Christopher Wren was among a number of famous men who felt the master's lash in their early days.

Like all dictators, Busby would accept no argument or criticism – when one of his fellow schoolmasters questioned the doctor's judgment, Busby sent a team of schoolboys with axes to chop down the staircase leading to the rebellious teacher's apartments. The teacher was left with no choice but to recant before being allowed to shin down a rope.

When at last old age had taken its toll and Busby was forced out and replaced by Dr Friend, the following verses were being chanted all over Westminster:

Ye sons of Westminster who still retain
Your ancient dread of Busby's awful reign
Forget at length your fears, your panic end –
The monarch of the place is now a friend!

Two of the best stories about Busby concern his extraordinary sense of his own importance. On the first occasion he welcomed Charles II to Westminster School but refused to doff his hat to the king – an extremely daring omission which at that sensitive time (so soon after the Restoration) could have had serious repercussions. When he was upbraided by the king, Busby is said to have replied: 'I cannot do it, for the boys would then think there is someone greater than I ...'

On another occasion Busby was discussing the role of headmaster with someone who suggested that it was perhaps a role of relatively little importance. Busby would have none of it and replied: 'The fathers of my boys rule the country. The mothers rule the fathers. The boys rule the mothers and I rule the boys.'

HOW TO AVOID DEBT
IN THE MALL

1661

The phrase 'shopping mall' is either greeted with horror or delight depending on one's attitude to a phenomenon that spread across town centres in America and then the UK like a plague (or a blessing) but the origins of the word mall lie deep in the history of central London, where The Mall and Pall Mall commemorate a game that has vanished as completely as the dodo.

The Mall referred originally to a strange game imported from Italy. The game *pallo a maglio* soon became known in English as 'pall mall'. It was played on a half-mile (800m) course laid out by James I and Charles I. The two kings were enthusiastic players and the game involved using sticks rather like hockey sticks to knock a ball along the course.

When the first course was destroyed as houses were put up along The Mall Charles II needed a new course. He built it on the north side of what is now The Mall. The old course became what we now call Pall Mall.

Because the king played the game crowds of wealthy Londoners and courtiers came regularly to watch the matches. The great diarist Samuel Pepys records seeing the king play in 1661.

'While the fashionable strollers watched they meandered up and down talking and enjoying the view across the park.' The area where pall mall was played also had the great advantage that being within the jurisdiction of the court of St James it was not subject to the debtors laws that applied everywhere else. This meant that in addition to fashionable promenaders The Mall attracted those who could not pay their debts. As long as they stayed there they could not be arrested. Soon the word 'mall' came to mean any fashionable place to promenade and loiter whether for conversation, exercise, shopping or debt avoidance!

Technically, even today, you still can't be arrested for debt if you are within the jurisdiction of St James's – but don't rely on it!

WHERE TO GET YOUR COAT OF ARMS

1666

The British are obsessed with social class – it's a truism but one that reverberates through history. In earlier times the rising middle classes tried desperately to find an ancestor or two who would introduce a hint of blue blood to the family. Thomas Hardy's *Tess of the D'Urbervilles* reveals that even a poor country girl could be fooled into thinking that her ancestors were aristocrats and that somehow this meant her whole life should change. Then there was Shakespeare, who made every effort to persuade the College of Arms to accept his family's entitlement to a banner that would proclaim them gentlemen through and through. He failed but the institution to which he applied for his coat of arms still exists in the heart of London.

The vast mystery of family coats of arms, their history, design, conception and meaning, can be traced to an ancient, crooked, but still magnificent building in Queen Victoria Street in the heart of the old City and close to the river.

A miraculous survivor of German bombs, the seventeenth-century College of Arms is home to a bizarre range of officials who can be grouped into the royal heralds and the kings at arms. There are three kings at arms – Garter, Norroy and Clarenceux. The royal heralds are York, Lancaster, Windsor, Chester, Somerset and Richmond. The college also houses the pursuivants – Rouge Dragon,

Blue Mantle, Rouge Croix and Portcullis. Each of these titles is given to one man. Bizarrely, the head of the college – the Earl Marshall – is always the Duke of Norfolk. Norfolk is England's premier dukedom but the family has always traditionally been Catholic and at least one had his head lopped off for treachery.

The role, complexity and purpose of the various jobs carried out at the College of Arms would take a whole book to explain but suffice it to say that even today, more than five centuries after the college was established, no one, whether company or individual, is allowed to design and use a coat of arms without the permission of the college and there are strict rules about what exactly can appear on a coat of arms. There are a number of cases where those who broke the rules have been fined heavily for so doing.

Most of the terms used by the college are based on a curious medieval mix of Norman French (still current in elevated circles for a century and more after the Norman invasion), Latin and Middle English.

The College of Arms still has the charters and other documentation that survived the Great Fire of 1666 when the fifteenth-century building on the same site was burned down. All the paperwork was bundled into a boat and taken across the river.

Traditionally – though this is apparently not the case now – jobs in the college were given to important friends of important people, which may explain the long line of eccentrics, drunks and lunatics who have snoozed away the decades in the ancient panelled rooms of this delightful building.

Among the most eccentric was William Oldys (1696– 1761), apparently given a job as herald because the Duke of Norfolk had enjoyed reading Oldys's book about Sir Walter Raleigh. Dukes of Norfolk, remember, always get the job of Earl Marshall, whose main role is to organise state occasions – funerals, weddings and coronations. Oldys spent his days and evenings in a local pub but employed a man to carry him back – completely drunk – to the college before midnight. If he was later than that it meant a fine. Oldys is best remembered today for a strange little poem he wrote towards the end of his life:

Busy curious thirsty fly
Drink with me and drink as I.
Freely welcome to my cup
Couldst thou sip and sip it up.
Make the most of life you may
Life is short and wears away.

A PITCHED BATTLE WITH
THE LAWYERS
1684

Whatever one thinks about youngsters misbehaving today – whether they are fighting in the streets, getting drunk or stealing cars – we should remember that it was at least as bad, if not far worse, in medieval and later London.

Endless ordinances were issued against London apprentices who regularly fought pitched battles against each other – the problem was exacerbated by the intense rivalry between the various guilds who taught their mysteries (their crafts) to apprentices who signed up for a period of training in medicine, leather work or any of the many other trades on which London depended.

But the London mob, as it was known, was even more fearsome than the unruly apprentices. The mob rose whenever rumour ran through the city that foreigners were up to no good (foreigners were periodically attacked and sometimes even killed) but one of the most bizarre uprisings occurred in 1684 after Nicolas Barbon, the famous property developer, bought the land that is now covered by Red Lion Square a little to the north of Holborn.

Barbon had grown rich building houses for the newly emerging middle classes – tradesmen and sometimes minor aristocrats who needed to live in or near London but wanted a fashionable address. In earlier periods (unlike today) older houses were shunned in favour of modern new houses – a complete reversal of the current situation where period houses invariably command a premium.

Problems arose when the lawyers of nearby Gray's Inn decided that the last thing they wanted was a new housing development on what was then open land to the west of their inn. Thinking the law would invariably side with them, the lawyers of Gray's Inn went to court to block Barbon's development but since, then as now, property was nine-tenths of the law, Barbon won. He won because he had bought the land fair and square.

But the lawyers refused to give up and when Barbon's workmen began digging the foundations of his new houses the lawyers, several hundred of them, ran out brandishing sticks and clubs and the workmen fled. The lawyers then filled in the trenches dug for the new houses and retreated to their inn.

Refusing to be beaten, Barbon hired several dozen of London's nastiest thugs along with a new batch of workmen. He began work again on the foundations. His heavies hid under tarpaulins in the workmen's carts and when the lawyers rushed out again the toughs jumped out of the wagons and a running fight began that lasted for most of the morning.

The lawyers, being essentially desk johnnies, were no match for the professional toughs and Barbon won the day. The lawyers had to accept defeat and Red Lion Square was built. Only one or two houses – much altered – survive from Barbon's time.

A MOUSETRAP ON THE HEAD

1690

Until the 1980s there was still a strange little jewellery shop tucked away in a corner of one of the ancient Inns of Court. The shop, known as the Silver Mousetrap, had traded continually from these premises since 1690, but if the survival of a shop that long in London is remarkable then the origin of the shop's name is even more noteworthy.

The name dates back to a time when rich, fashionable women would spend a day or two having their hair turned into an extraordinary sculpture. First the hair would be piled as high as possible – perhaps with the addition of artificial hair – and then plaster birds might be added to make it look as if birds were nesting in the hair and perhaps a small carved ship or a tree or simply a mass of artificial flowers. Occasionally a mix of all these things and more would be built into the structure of the hair, which was stiffened with flour, chalk dust or arsenic powder.

The problem with these fabulous creations is that they took so long to make that they had to be slept in for weeks at a time and until the style was changed the hair could not be washed. This led to a serious problem with mice.

Today, when we have a range of sophisticated chemicals to control mice and other pests, it is difficult to imagine what it was like when there were no really effective ways to control mice, rats, bedbugs and fleas – beds were routinely infested with bugs until the twentieth century and houses collapsed when wood-boring insects had done their work for long enough; walls and ceiling voids were commonly filled with mice which people tended to ignore, since the business of trying to remove or kill them was simply impossible. Even if it had been possible to eliminate a particular infestation newcomers would soon move in to take their place.

When a woman of fashion slept with her enormous head of firmly fixed hair mice invariably found their way into it, and even for a population that had learned to put up with the presence of various rodents this was too much.

For a woman embarrassed at the prospect of a mouse popping out of her hair during lunch or supper there was only one solution. A trip to The Silver Mousetrap, where elegant ladylike mousetraps made in silver were available. Having bought two or three of these things the woman of fashion, on retiring for the night, would place them strategically around her head. If the mice came out while she slept they would with any luck be caught in one or other of the traps. Users were warned not to roll about too much in their sleep lest an unwary nose or ear set off one of the traps!

WHEN PRISON MARRIAGES WERE ALL THE RAGE

1696

It is hard to believe now but 15 per cent of all marriages conducted in Britain during most of the late seventeenth and early eighteenth centuries were actually conducted in London's Fleet Prison, or more precisely in what were known as the Rules of the Fleet – an area bounded roughly by Fleet Lane, the Old Bailey, Farringdon Street and Ludgate Hill.

Today almost none of the maze of alleys and courtyards that once existed here survive. But in the eighteenth century the mass of cheap lodging houses within the Rules of the Fleet provided homes for Fleet prisoners who'd been given special privileges.

The Fleet was a debtors' prison but, under rules that dated back to medieval times, debtors who provided suitable security were let out of the prison itself on the understanding that they would not leave the Rules of the Fleet. Here they could live and carry on their jobs and professions until such time as their debts had been paid and they were released. But within the Rules imprisoned clergymen (and there were a surprisingly large number of imprisoned clergymen) were permitted to conduct entirely legal marriages.

The first Fleet marriage of which records survive took place in 1613 but by the late seventeenth century an odd ecclesiastical law meant that there was an explosion in the number of marriages carried out in the Fleet.

In 1696 the law changed so that clergymen who married couples without first declaring the banns were prosecuted – as they were beneficed clergymen they might lose their livings. Clergymen in the Fleet were by definition unbeneficed (i.e. they had no parishes) and could not therefore be prosecuted as the law specifically referred to beneficed clergymen, so anyone who wanted to marry without their parents' permission could do so only at the Fleet.

Couples arrived in their hundreds and then thousands and there was little the authorities could do. Some have argued that the authorities deliberately left this loophole open to reduce the number of illicit relationships.

As well as within the prison itself, Fleet marriages took place in coffee houses, lodging rooms and shops of all kinds (from booksellers to bakers). What's more, it was possible to be married at any time of the day or night, seven days a week throughout the year – the Fleet in early eighteenth-century London had the sort of reputation for marriages that Las Vegas has today.

More than 250,000 couples are recorded as marrying in the Fleet before the rules changed and the prison was demolished – some of the marriages were no doubt forced or fraudulent but many couples' motives were entirely honourable. They were merely attracted by the speed and relative cheapness of a Fleet marriage.

THE BOARD OF THE GREEN CLOTH

1698

After a disastrous fire in 1698 that almost completely destroyed the old Palace of Westminster, the monarch and his courtiers moved away, never to return. The Palace – more a collection of haphazard buildings – had covered all the ground from Westminster Hall, which survived the fire, to well beyond the Banqueting House, the only other major part of the old palace that survived the fire.

In other words the old palace covered much of the road still known as Whitehall today as well as all the land running from it down to the river.

Because it was home to the king and his court, this area was treated as rather special in every respect, and this has led to one of London's strangest survivals – a government body known as the Board of Green Cloth.

Named after the cloth covering over the table at which it met, the Board of Green Cloth was set up while the court was still at Whitehall and before the fire with the express purpose of licensing pubs, theatres and other places of entertainment within what was known in seventeenth-century England as the Verge of the Court. This meant anywhere within the Palace of Whitehall precincts – and remember taverns could be set up within the precincts of the palace as it was more like a village spread over a wide area than a palace in the sense we understand that term today. But the Verge of the Court also included the area around Whitehall extending well beyond the limits of the palace – but precisely how much of this outside area was defined as being within the Verge of the Court has never really been established.

The strangest thing about the Board of the Green Cloth is that it existed until reforms brought about by the Licensing Act of 2003 and until that time, if you applied for a licence for a pub or theatre within the area of its ancient jurisdiction, you still had to prove to the board you were a fit person to work within the bounds of a court that vanished more than three centuries ago.

PIG FAT
AND FACE POWDER
1700

Among the dottiest people who ever lived in London was Lady Lewson, famed throughout the middle decades of the eighteenth century for her bizarre lifestyle.

Records suggest she was born in 1700 or perhaps 1701 in Essex Street just north of the Strand. Mrs Lewson – or Lady Lewson as she was afterwards known – married a rich elderly merchant when she was just 19 and moved to his house at Clerkenwell, then a quiet village on the edge of London.

Her husband died when she was only 26, but from that time until her death in about 1800, she hardly ever left the house. Every day she made sure all the beds in the house were made up, although no one ever came to stay. She was highly superstitious: in over 60 years she never cleaned a window in the house, fearing they would be broken in the process or that the person cleaning them might be injured. And she refused to allow anything to be moved in any room, believing that it might make her catch cold.

In summer she was sometimes seen reading in her garden in attire which would have been far more appropriate to the fashion of about 1690, with 'ruffs and cuffs and fardingales', and she always wore her hair powdered and piled high on her head over a stiff horsehair frame.

She believed washing was highly dangerous and would lead to some 'dreadful disorder'. Instead she smeared her face and neck with pig's fat, on top of which she applied a liberal quantity of pink powder.

When Lady Lewson died it was the talk of London – her house was opened up to mourners and the curious who found a time capsule unchanged in more than 70 years.

THE CANDLE-STUB
SELLER
1707

Very few of London's shops last more than a century, but at least one is far older than that and the story of its origins is both strange and fascinating. Most shops survive by adapting and constantly modernising but Fortnum & Mason has in many ways done just the opposite.

One of the last of London's truly old-fashioned stores, Fortnum's still insists that the staff in its wine shop should wear frock coats.

The shop's origins lie in the friendship between William Fortnum, a footman in the royal household, and Hugh Mason, a shopkeeper. As a footman to Queen Anne, one of Fortnum's jobs was to ensure that the candles in the palace candelabra were regularly replaced. He was allowed the stumps of the old candles and sold these on – candles were very expensive in the eighteenth century and William did a roaring trade with his candle-stump business, though the stumps were mostly sold to the very poor.

Over the years he spent working in the royal household at St James's Palace, William learned just how a big house was run, so when he retired he suggested to his friend John Mason that they set up a shop together supplying the nearby palace and the gentry right across Mayfair and Piccadilly.

The shop, opened near the premises it still occupies today, did so well that the two men quickly expanded the business and bought a big team of horses and carts for deliveries.

By the beginning of the nineteenth century Fortnum and Mason were famous for importing a vast range of wonderfully exotic foods – many never seen before in England – from the East, largely through the East India Company which was expanding rapidly at that time.

Explorers and generals took Fortnum's potted meats and other foods with them and soon the shop's hampers were being sent all over the world – Queen Victoria famously sent a huge Fortnum's vat of beef tea to Florence Nightingale (1820–1910) in the Crimea and the explorer William Parry (1790–1855) set off in search of the North West Passage in 1819 with a casket of more than two hundredweight (102kg) of Fortnum and Mason cocoa powder!

Sadly Fortnum and Mason's beautiful old shop was rebuilt in the 1920s, but an elaborate clock made in the 1960s and fitted to the Piccadilly front of the store commemorates its Georgian origins. It shows the figures of Mr Fortnum and Mr Mason and when the clock strikes the hour the two figures step out and bow to each other. The figure in the red coat is Fortnum – red being the colour of the dress of footmen of the royal household.

Traditions in the shop also hark back two centuries and more – the man in charge of the bakery, for example, is known even today as the 'Groom of the Pastry'.

THE CHURCH THAT WENT TO AMERICA

1724

The early churches of New England and indeed across America are much admired for the simple elegance of their design, but it is a little-known fact that their design is based almost entirely on London's St Martin-in-the-Fields.

What sounds delightfully eccentric today refers to the fact that when the church was completed in 1724 it stood in agricultural land on the edge of the village of Charing – in other words it really was in the fields rather than in the town.

But St Martin's shocked the citizens of London because however traditional it may now look it was revolutionary in eighteenth-century eyes. Until it was built it was accepted practice to place the steeple at the east end of the church not the west end, but architect James Gibbs (1682–1754) decided to turn the thing on its head and build the steeple where we see it today. He also built it above an imposing portico that looks like the grand entrance to an ancient temple.

Critics and architects marvelled at the audaciousness of the new church and despite the innate conservatism of churchgoers and the church authorities the new design soon became very popular – so much so that several members of Gibbs's architectural practice were enticed to America by the offer of large sums of money. With the design of St Martin's packed in their saddle bags they moved west as the American settlers moved west, building identical or near identical copies of St Martin's as they went.

GOING TO
KNIGHTSBRIDGE
BY BOAT

1736

The Serpentine Lake in Hyde Park is one of London's best-known landmarks. It has an unusual history in that it was originally not a lake at all but a stretch of one of London's many small rivers, each a tributary of the Thames.

Just outside the western wall of the old City of London was the Fleet River, which ran down what is now Farringdon Street through Ludgate Circus and thence into the Thames. Further west, but again running north–south, the Tyburn flowed down what is now Edgware Road on through Victoria and parallel with Vauxhall Bridge Road before reaching the Thames.

The Westbourne flowed from Hampstead Heath down through west London and across Hyde Park, down modern Sloane Street and across Sloane Square before reaching the Thames just to the east of Christopher Wren's magnificent Chelsea Hospital.

It was Charlotte, George II's queen, who decided that Hyde Park needed a great lake. The park itself had been the property of the Crown since Henry VIII took it from the monks of Westminster in 1536 (the monks had in their turn no doubt taken it from someone else) to use as a hunting ground. The public at this time were strictly forbidden to enter the park.

Early in the seventeenth century James I allowed limited access to the park but only for the nobility and aristocracy.

Charles I opened the park to the public in 1637 and created The Ring – the sandy road that allowed the fashionable for the next three centuries to parade and be seen on foot and on horseback and in their carriages.

Queen Charlotte decided the lake would make the park far more attractive so the River Westbourne was dammed and excavations began to produce the splendid stretch of water we see today.

But the first phase of the work left the River Westbourne flowing above ground as a way to control the level in the lake. In 1736 a massive flood led to the Westbourne bursting its banks and the whole of the area south of the Serpentine down through the Albert Gate, through Knightsbridge and Belgravia was under several feet of water for weeks. The Thames watermen made the most of an opportunity and rowed sightseers from Chelsea up to Knightsbridge and beyond. At this time most of the roads around London were impassable to wheeled vehicles for most of the year anyway so the sudden appearance of extra water for boat travel – always the preferred mode of transport for Londoners – made Hyde Park far more popular than it would otherwise have been.

MAD MAYFAIR MARRIAGES

1742

Mayfair was once a rather sleazy area and certainly nothing like the millionaires' quarter it has now become. Something of its less salubrious past can be discovered in Shepherd Market where prostitutes still ply their trade, but more or less exclusively for the well to do.

But Mayfair was also once home to one of London's strangest churches. Until the Marriage Act of 1754, the Mayfair chapel was a continual thorn in the side of the authorities – it was here that the eccentric clergyman, the Reverend Alexander Keith, conducted marriage ceremonies for anyone who turned up at any time of day or night and absolutely no questions asked.

For the church and secular authorities of the eighteenth century, churchmen just didn't do this sort of thing, but if the clergyman was properly ordained there was very little anyone could do to stop it.

For young runaways and the romantically inclined, in an age when marriages were largely a matter of convenience, financial or otherwise, the Mayfair chapel was a godsend.

The authorities hated it because it represented a threat to the financial and dynastic plans they had for their own offspring, but Alexander Keith knew the law and he was perfectly entitled to do what he was doing. The popularity of the Mayfair chapel can be judged by the fact that in just one year – 1742 – he married no fewer than 70 couples –

and all with neither licence nor banns. Parliament launched several attempts to change the law to make these marriages illegal but they immediately abandoned the attempt when they realised – the Lords particularly – that to do so would be to make many of their own nephews, nieces and grandchildren illegitimate.

Among the most famous marriages conducted at the Mayfair chapel was that between the Duke of Hamilton and Elizabeth Dunning, one of the great beauties of Georgian England. The couple were in such a hurry that an old brass washer had to be used in place of a gold band.

GOING IN DISGUISE

1750

James Gray returned to London from service with the Navy in the Far East in 1750. Gray – who was known as Hearty Jemmy – was notorious for fighting and drinking, but within a few weeks of his return he was exposed as a fraud, for James Gray was not a man at all: he was a widow called Hannah Snell.

Hannah admitted having shared a room and a bed with dozens of male comrades in arms without once being discovered.

During her military career – which had lasted for more than five years – she had been wounded several times and flogged for various misdemeanours. It seems hard to credit but despite all this and more her identity as a woman was never even suspected. It was only after she had retired with a war pension that her secret was finally disclosed – and she was the one who disclosed it. But her years of deception paid off because she had a second career as a theatrical performer – she danced and sang for many years at London's Sadler's Wells theatre where she was the star attraction dressed in full military regalia.

But her story starts in Worcester where she was born in 1723. By the age of 23 she was married to a Dutch seaman. It was a big mistake and within a year he had deserted her.

But Hannah was not one to take desertion lying down – she wanted to catch up with her errant husband and decided the best way to do it was to join the Navy herself. She borrowed her cousin's clothes and his name and enlisted in 1745 in Guise's Regiment of Foot.

Hannah was signed on without question simply because, at that time, no one would have dreamed that a woman would even consider doing such a thing.

Within months and following a flogging for insubordination Hannah deserted the army and joined the Navy instead. She signed up at Portsmouth. Clearly a bit of a rebel she was quickly in trouble and flogged again but she stayed at sea and by all accounts proved a remarkably brave fighter.

She was involved in hand to hand fighting during one skirmish just outside Madras in India, she dug trenches and latrines, waded through rivers and was wounded more than a dozen times.

Sometime later, no one is sure exactly when, she sailed for Lisbon where she heard news that her husband had been executed. She refused to leave the Navy until her five years were up and she could claim her pension, which is exactly what she did.

When she finally returned to London with her money she had her story printed and became the talk of the town. The Duke of Cumberland was so impressed he put her name on the King's List (a list of pensioners) to receive £30 a year.

She eventually married again and opened a pub in Wapping called The Female Warrior but, for reasons that have never been explained, she ended her days in the Bethlehem Hospital for the insane. She died there in 1792.

ABSENT-MINDED ECCENTRIC

1755

Educated at Oxford, the Revd George Harvest first tried to become an actor. When that failed he took holy orders in 1755 and decided to get married, but he was so forgetful that when the great day dawned he went fishing, not returning until nightfall. Only then did he remember he should have been at the village church.

His life as a churchman was filled with bizarre behaviour – so much so that he came close to being de-frocked on a number of occasions.

He was the parish priest of Thames Ditton on the edge of modern London for more than 30 years, and in that time turned absentmindedness into an art form. But despite his extraordinary forgetfulness – which infuriated his superiors – he was a goodhearted man and much liked by his congregation, something that probably accounts for the fact that he managed to keep his job for so long.

Often when he wrote a letter he would write it to one person, address it to a second, and post it to a third. Paying a visit to London on one occasion he passed a beggar in the street, and when the beggar raised his hat in hopes of being given a penny, Harvest was in such a dream that he merely thought it was an acquaintance and raised his hat in return.

When he needed to travel he invariably had to borrow a horse, for he mislaid his own horses after a few days. But he had a terrible tendency to lose borrowed horses too, and eventually no one would lend him a horse no matter how dire the emergency.

Whenever he had dinner at a friend's house he would try to leave by going up instead of downstairs, and he invariably got lost on the way home. He often went into his neighbour's house at night thinking he was at home, and would then be found fast asleep in the wrong bed.

Towards the end of his life he made a second marriage proposal and was accepted. On the day of the wedding he woke early, and finding the weather wonderful he wandered off to Richmond and then Kew where he met some friends and passed a delightful day without so much as a glimmer of memory that his bride-to-be and her family would be waiting for him some miles off.

On another occasion in a box watching a play in the Haymarket he leant forward too far and his old and very grubby nightcap fell off his head and into the theatre pit, where it was thrown backwards and forwards by the audience. Afraid it would never be returned to him, Harvest stood up in the middle of the play and preached for ten minutes, concluding that 'it is a very serious thing to die without a nightcap'. To which he added: 'I shall be restless tonight if 1 have not my cap'. The audience was stunned by his serious manner and the cap was handed back up to him on the end of a stick.

At a grand dinner in Park Lane with Lady Onslow and a number of distinguished guests he spotted a large fly on his neighbour's bonnet. He leapt to his feet and shouted 'May you be married!' at the top of his voice and struck the woman a violent blow on the head. In fact he hit her so hard he knocked her out. He was never invited to dinner again. He died in 1789.

AIR BATHING
IN CRAVEN STREET
1757

It's a little-known fact that Benjamin Franklin (1706–90), one of the four men who signed the American Declaration of Independence, lived for 16 years in a crooked little terraced house in Craven Street, a street that, before the building of the Embankment in the 1860s, ran down to the mud banks of the River Thames.

Craven Street survived the building of the Embankment – which effectively pushed the river back 200 yards (183m) – as well as the building of Charing Cross Station, the German bombs of the Second World War and the obsession with redevelopment in the 1960s. Virtually all the houses in the street are eighteenth century although most have been over-restored to create office space.

No. 36, Franklin's old home, is one of the few to survive with its interior virtually intact – what we see today are the doors, chimneypieces and staircases once used by Franklin himself and it was here that Franklin pursued some of his more eccentric interests.

Franklin was a great friend of Erasmus Darwin (1731–1802), Matthew Boulton (1728–1809) and Josiah Wedgwood (1730–95), all members of the Lunar Society, a Midlands-based dining club of industrialists and engineers who embraced every new invention of the late eighteenth century – the first great period of the Industrial Revolution.

Franklin was passionate about science long before he became passionate about American politics. He was also a noted eccentric and if you had wandered along Craven Street early in the eighteenth century on a summer's day you might easily have seen Franklin sitting in his downstairs drawing-room window completely naked!

He was a great believer in the medical benefits of what was then called 'Air bathing' – a form of recreation to which William Blake (1757–1827) was also partial in the garden of his house across the river in Lambeth.

Franklin was also fascinated by electricity, dentistry, chemistry and optics. Like his friends in the Birmingham factories he believed that science would lead to a better life for mankind. He was also keen on practical experiments. He was part of that group of inventors who organised public demonstrations of electricity by spinning a glass ball against a leather pad to produce a huge build-up of static. As one contemporary put it: 'Franklin is a lightning rod philosopher who goes to the Charterhouse School each week, catches a charity boy, strings him up on silk cords, rubs him with glass and extracts sparks from his nose.'

Franklin's other exploits included swimming in the Thames at Chelsea on his back while paring his nails. He did it just to prove it could be done and he also had a set of wooden false teeth made.

The great radical writer William Cobbett (1763–1835) disliked Franklin, describing him as 'That crafty and lecherous old hypocrite', but he was much loved by his Birmingham industrialist friends.

When his house in Craven Street was being restored in the 1990s a mass of human bones was found buried in the basement – at first the police suspected a serial killer but it turns out that Franklin lodged with William Hewson, a doctor who ran an anatomy school from the Craven Street house. The bones showed evidence of surgery – skulls had been trepanned, for example, and leg bones mended.

But whatever went on in this particular house we know there was a roaring trade in corpses in eighteenth-century London. The 'resurrection men', as those who stole bodies from graveyards were known, would have rowed to the river steps at the bottom of Craven Street before delivering their gruesome cargo – human bones from babies, teenagers, the middle aged and elderly were all found buried here. The other source of at least some of these bones would have been the gallows that then stood just behind the garden wall of No. 30.

While he lived at Craven Street, Franklin complained about the smoky fire in his rooms – the metal damper he invented to solve the problem still exists in the house.

Before the Embankment was built Craven Street ran down to the edge of the Thames and, like the Londoners of old, you can still take a boat from here to the Tower of London or to Greenwich. Famous residents included Henrich Heine (1797–1856), the German poet, and Grinling Gibbons (1648–1721), the great woodcarver.

The author James Smith wrote a splendid satirical poem about the lawyers who were his neighbours in the street during the early nineteenth century:

In Craven Street Strand, ten attorneys find place
And ten dark coal barges are moored at its base.
Fly honesty Fly, seek some safer retreat
For there's craft in the river and craft in the street.

A poetical lawyer responded with the following verse:

Why should honesty fly to some safer retreat
From attorneys and barges god rot 'em
For the lawyers are just at the top of the street
And the barges are just at the bottom.

Benjamin Franklin's house – the scene of so many of these bizarre tales – is now open to the public having recently been beautifully restored.

HIGHLAND SOIL IN
WESTMINSTER

1760

The British are notoriously eccentric and as a general rule it is probably pretty safe to say that the richer the individual the greater the eccentricity. One of the most eccentric London residents of all time has to be the eighteenth-century Earl of Fife. A staunch Jacobite who hated the repression of the Scots that followed their defeat at Culloden in 1745, he was determined to get the better of the English whenever he could.

But the Earl was in a tricky position – from 1760 on he found that he had to visit London regularly for business reasons and the easiest way to do this, then as now for the very rich, was to buy or build a house. But the Earl's motives were not entirely financial – he hated the idea of being in London at all and by building his own house he could avoid the horror of having to stay in an English hotel run by the hated English.

But even if he built his own house in London it would still be on English soil, which was anathema to the good Earl. His solution was to buy a plot of land on Horse Guards Avenue near Whitehall. He then arranged, at enormous expense, to have a merchant ship filled with Scottish soil and sailed down the coast and up the Thames to Whitehall Steps. From here the soil was carried up Whitehall in a series of carts and dumped on the Earl's new acre of ground. Once the detested English soil had been completely covered with far superior Scottish soil the Earl went ahead and built his new house.

Sadly not a trace of that house remains today; but since we have no evidence that the soil beneath the house was ever removed we must assume that the land here is still as Scottish as it was in 1760.

HOW LONDON GOT ITS PAVEMENTS

1761

Near the top of Whitehall, a hundred yards or so from Trafalgar Square where Nelson looks down from his column towards Westminster Abbey and the Houses of Parliament, there is a little-known alleyway.

Few Londoners ever bother with it, let alone visitors, but it has a history as rich and interesting as many of London's better-known landmarks.

Walking down from Trafalgar Square, Craig's Court is a narrow alley to the left. It runs into a small square or court where the façade of Harrington House, built in 1702 for the Earl of Harrington, still stands, though it has been remodelled over the centuries. The Earl built his house here just a few years after a huge fire destroyed the medieval palace of Whitehall.

Harrington was convinced that Whitehall Palace would be rebuilt, so it must have seemed logical that if his family lived right next to it – overlooking it in fact – they would be perfectly poised to visit the court every day and seek patronage. Patronage meant titles or jobs in the king's gift that entitled the holder to an income, but required little or no work of him. It was a system that, by the beginning of the nineteenth century, was known as Old Corruption, but in the mid-eighteenth century it was just the way things were done.

As it turned out, Harrington was wrong and the palace was

never rebuilt, so he sat in his huge house with Parliament half a mile (800m) away at the other end of Whitehall.

A more curious tale than the history of the house is the history of the alleyway beside it, because this is where London's pavements began.

Until the mid-eighteenth century, London's streets had no pavements at all. In other words there was no physical distinction between that part of the roadway where wheeled vehicles travelled and that part where pedestrians walked. Whenever the cart and carriage drivers wanted to they would drive along the streets as near to the walls of the houses as they liked. This meant that going for a walk was a dangerous business, particularly when you remember that eighteenth-century London had far fewer wide streets than it does today. It also meant that in particularly narrow streets, carriages occasionally got stuck – quite literally – between the houses.

Kerbstones and pavements began to appear after the Speaker of the House of Commons, Mr Speaker Onslow, got stuck in Craig's Court after a visit to Harrington's house.

Parliament had long debated what to do about the narrow, dirty, dangerous streets of London, but they could never reach agreement about who should pay for improvements. Then one day early in the 1760s Onslow drove in his massive, stately carriage up Whitehall and into Craig's Court. At the narrowest part of the alleyway where it opens into the courtyard his carriage got stuck fast between the walls of the houses on either side. If there had been kerbstones and pavements the driver would have been stopped before he got stuck.

After fruitless attempts to extricate the carriage, a red-faced and by all accounts extremely angry Mr Speaker Onslow had to be extricated through a hole cut in the roof of the carriage.

He returned to Parliament on foot and when the next debate on the state of the streets was held he helped vote through a bill that compelled each householder in London to pay for a row of kerbstones in front of his or her house.

More early kerbstones can be seen if you retrace your steps down the narrow alleyway and out into Whitehall. If you cross the street and look at the kerbstones here (roughly in front of the 1930s theatre) you'll see several are marked with an arrow.

The mark was introduced by Elizabeth I to stop people stealing army and navy property and it is still used today. The pavement act of 1762 that made the Harringtons provide kerbstones in Craig's Court also obliged Admiralty officials to provide kerbstones outside their premises at the top of Whitehall. As they were Admiralty kerbstones they had to have the arrowhead mark which one or two retain to this day.

WHY ACTORS SAY 'BREAK A LEG!'

1766

The theatrical phrase 'break a leg!' – a good-luck wish before a performance – has its origins in a little-known but curiously endearing story from the Theatre Royal in the Haymarket.

When Samuel Foote (1720–77) took over the running of the theatre in the second half of the eighteenth century he knew he was taking a risk because the theatre, then known as the Little Theatre, did not have a licence – theatre licences could only be granted by the King and the King resolutely refused to grant the Little Theatre a licence because a previous owner had published a number of pamphlets attacking the government and the Crown.

Foote was undaunted and attempted by every means to obtain the necessary royal warrant but all to no avail. He found a way round the problem temporarily by not charging those who came to see his plays. Audiences could get in free but Foote made up for what he failed to take at the door by charging hugely inflated prices for coffee and food during the intervals.

This infuriated the Crown and made it less likely that Foote would ever get the royal seal of approval, but a bizarre turn of events changed all that. The King's brother, the Duke of York, overheard Foote boasting about his horsemanship and challenged him to ride with him the following morning. Foote agreed but the Duke deliberately brought a horse that had never been ridden. Foote inevitably was thrown and badly injured – he broke a leg and spent weeks recovering. The Duke was stricken with remorse and to make up for what he had done he granted Foote the royal licence for which he had waited so long. It was 1766 and the Little Theatre in the Haymarket became the Theatre Royal, a title it has enjoyed uninterrupted ever since. The phrase 'break a leg' passed into the language – a sign that present disaster can quickly be transformed into future success.

BYRON GETS BURNED

1768

Albemarle Street just off Piccadilly was for more than two centuries the home of one of the world's most extraordinary publishers: John Murray, who came to London in 1768 to seek his fortune.

Born in 1739 he was originally John McMurray but dropped the 'Mc' on coming to London after a number of years' service as a lieutenant in the marines. Murray's first office was in Fleet Street where, quite by chance, he took over No. 32, the site of Wynkyn de Word's printing press established in 1500. But within a few years he had moved to 50 Albemarle Street from which office, among a host of dazzling writers, the firm published David Hume, Byron, Jane Austen, Charles Darwin, Gladstone and Sir Arthur Conan Doyle.

By 2005 – some 230 years later – the firm was still being run from this small house at 50 Albemarle Street, making it the oldest independent book publisher in the world. The original fireplaces were still here until the company was finally sold in 2003; the alcoves and odd corners remain in what is still in essence an eighteenth-century house.

Little had changed in more than two centuries by the time the company was sold and, most astonishing of all, the firm was always run by a John Murray – the last was the seventh direct male descendant of the founder.

It was only when the seventh John Murray's two sons

(neither incidentally called John) decided they did not want to go into the family business that the firm was reluctantly sold to a huge multinational whose name – for the sake of decency – had probably better not be mentioned.

There are moves to make 50 Albemarle Street into a museum but in the meantime the company's archives – thousands of letters and other documents relating to its history and the host of famous authors it published – are likely to be sold, at the time of writing, for as much as £40 million. Most of the material has never been catalogued or seen.

Everything to do with John Murray is remarkable but most intriguing of all was a meeting that took place in 1824 in an upstairs room in front of a fireplace that is still there. John Murray the second met with the executors of Byron's estate shortly after the poet's death. They held in their hands two manuscript volumes of the great poet's diaries but they were so scandalised by the contents that they decided to throw them on the fire and thus was lost for ever what would have been one of the greatest literary treasures of the Romantic age. Perhaps, too, the publisher was getting his revenge on the poet who would often arrive in the office and while talking to Murray would practise his fencing by lunging at the various books around the room and tearing holes in them with his sword!

OBSESSED BY SNUFF

1776

Today drug taking is frowned on by the respectable, but in earlier times there was no stigma attached to those who took opium – famous drug-addict authors like Thomas de Quincey (whose *Confessions of an English Opium Eater* was published in 1821), poets such as Samuel Taylor Coleridge and members of the royal family were enthusiastic drug takers and they would have laughed at the idea that taking opium was somehow a bad thing. However, opium was always the drug of choice for the relatively well off – lower down the social scale, the most popular drug of all before cigarettes was snuff. Snuff taking was almost universal in Georgian and Victorian England, but few were as enthusiastic about powdered tobacco as the infamous Margaret Thomson.

When she made her will in the early part of the nineteenth century Mrs Thomson, who lived in Essex Street just off the Strand, stipulated that the beneficiaries of her will would not get a penny if they failed to ensure that her coffin was filled with all the snuff handkerchiefs that were unwashed at the time of her death; she also wanted to be surrounded with freshly ground snuff in her coffin. Six of the greatest snuff takers in the parish were requested to be her pallbearers, and each was asked to wear a snuff-coloured hat. Six girls were instructed to walk behind the hearse, each with a box of snuff which they were to take copiously for their refreshment as they went along.

The priest who officiated at the ceremony was invited to take as much snuff as he desired during the service, and Mrs Thomson left him five guineas on condition that he partook of snuff during and throughout the funeral proceedings.

In return for a bequest of snuff, her servants were instructed to walk in front of the funeral procession throwing snuff on the ground and on to the crowd of onlookers. And throughout the long day of the funeral, snuff was to be distributed to all comers from the door of the deceased's house.

HOW THE BRISTOL HOTEL
GOT ITS NAME
1778

London still has at least one Bristol Hotel – it is in Berkeley Street, W1 – but during the late eighteenth century the city boasted a profusion of hotels, all called Bristol. Outside London and indeed right across Europe the situation was the same. There were Bristol hotels wherever travellers tended to stop for the night.

The reason has to do with one of London's oddest characters – a man largely forgotten today but in his lifetime a byword for luxury and extravagance.

Born in 1730, Edward Hervey studied at Westminster and Cambridge. Through the influence of his brother, Lord Bristol, he was made Bishop of Cloyne, though as he himself admitted he had absolutely no connection with or interest in Ireland. However, he soon started manoeuvring for the bishopric of Derry, which was worth more money than Cloyne, again using the influence of his brother, and he was successful. When he heard the news he was playing leapfrog with his fellow clergy in the garden at Cloyne Palace and is reported to have shouted: 'I will jump no more, gentlemen. I have surpassed you all, and jumped from Cloyne to Derry!'

He was 39, married, and earning a reputation as an eccentric largely because he was sympathetic to the local Catholic population which, under English rule, could own virtually nothing nor hold any office of any worth. His outspokenness on the subject almost led to him being impeached for treason, and Walpole, Charles James Fox and most other English parliamentarians thought him mad, bad and dangerous to know.

He got nowhere with his radical views, however, and developed instead his personality. He built three huge houses, his favourite being the size of Blenheim Palace, perched on a cliff top at Lough Foyle. On the death of his brother in 1778 he became Lord Bristol and went to live in London.

His house parties – held in his huge London residence – were legendary; he would often invite the fattest clergy to stay and then, after dinner, make them race round the house against each other. If he invited the clergy wives he always sprinkled flour outside their bedroom doors to see if he could catch them moving about between bedrooms during the night.

In his latter years he rarely visited Ireland and spent most of his time getting drunk in London and travelling extensively in France and Italy, where he spent so lavishly that hotel owners vied with each other to make their hotels more attractive to the great man. Hundreds renamed their hotels after him in order to indicate to other potential customers that the great Lord Bristol had stayed there and dozens retain the name 'Bristol' to this day.

Towards the end of his life he received a 'round robin' criticising him for being absent for so long from his parish, but he sent each signatory an inflated pig's bladder containing a dried pea along with a copy of the following verse:

Three large bluebottles sat upon three bladders.
Blow bottle flies, blow; burst, blow bladder burst.
A new-blown bladder and three blue balls
Make a great rattle.
So rattle bladder rattle.

He died in 1803 aged 73.

EIGHTEENTH-CENTURY VIAGRA

1779

Dr James Graham was a genuine doctor, but at a time when all genuine doctors were by modern standards complete frauds – the evidence for this can be seen in the fact that, for example an Edinburgh medical textbook of 1750 listed under 'valuable remedies' the following: horse dung, pig skulls, frogspawn, ants' eggs and ground-up human skulls.

But Dr Graham, though interested in medicine, was far more interested in money, which is why, when he left his native Edinburgh for London in around 1774, he set up his surgery in the most fashionable part of town – St James.

By 1779 he had realised that an important medical affliction was not at that time being addressed. Dr Graham decided that he would corner the market in cures for infertility. He set up his Temple of Health in Pall Mall and took large expensive advertisements in the London newspapers. In these he made outlandish claims for the extraordinary benefits of what he called his 'Celestial Bed'. The idea was that infertile couples would seek out the doctor, ask his advice and then be directed to his own certain cure: the Celestial Bed. Not only would the bed cure infertility – it would also ensure that any children conceived on it were far stronger and more beautiful 'in mental as well as in bodily endowments than the present puny race of Christians'.

The bed could only be rented and couples paid exorbitant sums for the privilege – perhaps as much as £100 per session. Graham claimed that while an infertile couple had sex on his bed he would activate a mechanism that would surround the happy couple with 'celestial fire' and cherishing vapours. He would also pump through glass tubes the very same perfumes used by the Turkish Sultan to guarantee that he could keep up with the demands of his enormous harem.

Despite the bed's mattress being made from the baked tails of sexually rapacious 'English stallions', history does not record the levels of satisfaction enjoyed by Dr Graham's customers, but we do know that within a few years of the advertisements appearing the good doctor vanished from the London scene.

BEAU BRUMMEL'S
BLUE NOSE

1794

Beau Brummel (1778–1840), close friend of the Prince
Regent and arbiter of fashion in the early part of the
nineteenth century, had in his younger days been an officer
in the 10th Light Dragoons. When he wasn't soldiering he
lived in some splendour in a house in Chesterfield Street in
London's Mayfair, where he taught the Prince of Wales to
tie his own cravat (the prince never quite mastered the art)
and where endless numbers of the fashionable came to be
passed fit to be seen in society by the great arbiter of taste.

Brummel had been commissioned into the dragoons
by his friend the Prince Regent but despite his fashion
sense he was a hopeless incompetent when it came to
matters military, for Brummel was one of England's most
forgetful soldiers.

His biggest difficulty was that he could never remember
the faces of the men in the troop he commanded – it was a
chronic problem that led to huge embarrassment and there
seemed to be no solution but, then as now, incompetence
was no bar to high rank in the British army provided one
had the right accent and background, which of course
Brummel had.

Then Brummel himself came up with a solution – he
noticed that one of the men in his troop had a very blue
nose and he ordered that this man should always be in the
front rank when the men were assembled. If Brummel

then failed to identify his troop of men he would need only to look for that blue nose to know that he was in the right place.

All went well until one day at the Horse Guards in Whitehall. Brummel sat immaculately dressed on his splendid horse and was approached by a senior officer who demanded what he thought he was doing.

Brummel stared in blank amazement at the squadron commander. 'You are with the wrong troop,' he was told in no uncertain terms.

Panic-stricken, Brummel stared around and with a sigh of relief spotted the blue nose in the men lined up just in front of him.

'I think, if I may say so, you are mistaken,' he replied. 'I'm not so foolish as to be unable to recognise my own troop.' But what Brummel, who famously spent most of his army career in front of a mirror, did not know was that there had been a troop reorganisation and 'blue nose' had been moved to another troop without his knowledge.

BETTING ON CATS

1795

Bond Street is unusual in that unlike almost every other London district it has never lost its reputation as a fashionable place to shop. It's also unusual in that it is the only street that runs right across Mayfair from Piccadilly to Oxford Street. Despite this, the street is actually two streets – the southern section, which runs as far north as Burlington Gardens, was built in the early 1680s by Sir Thomas Bond, the northern section in the 1720s.

Most of the original seventeenth-and eighteenth-century houses have now gone (Aspreys' shop is an exception) but from the first the street was so popular as a shopping destination that it also became an important place simply to be seen, so much so that it began to rival both the famous pleasure gardens at Ranelagh and Rotten Row.

Among those who regularly promenaded here in the late eighteenth century was the Prince of Wales, later the Prince Regent. The prince was a notorious gambler who would bet on almost anything – he once took a bet on which of two raindrops would be first to run to the bottom of a window – but he was also something of a simpleton who was regularly fleeced by his gambling-mad courtiers.

The politician Charles James Fox (1749–1806), a supporter of American independence, anti-slavery campaigner and Britain's first Foreign Secretary, once got the better of the Prince of Wales in a bizarre bet made while walking down

Bond Street one sunny afternoon. Fox noticed a cat lounging at the side of the street so he suggested to the Prince that each should choose one side of the street and then wager who would see the greatest number of cats during a walk from one end of the street to the other.

Fox was crafty enough to choose the side of the street in full sun rather than the shady side and at the end of their walk he had spotted 13 cats to the Prince's grand total of none. The baffled prince was forced to hand over the entire contents of his purse.

NELSON'S
SECOND-HAND TOMB

1805

Despite suffering almost continually from seasickness –
he never became a seasoned sailor – Nelson became the
greatest of all British naval heroes. It seems, too, almost as
if he knew that it was his duty to die in battle at sea, which
is of course precisely what happened.

But Nelson was so concerned that his death should be in
keeping with his life that he commissioned his own coffin
well in advance. Though it sounds rather ghoulish today
this was actually quite common in earlier times. Nelson
was very specific about his coffin – he had it made from the
salvaged timber of a French ship sunk at the Battle of the
Nile in 1798 and left strict instructions about what was to
be done in the event of his death.

When he was killed at Trafalgar in 1805 Britain lost its
greatest hero and looked around for a suitable way to bury
him. Clearly it had to be in St Paul's Cathedral and as he
had chosen his own coffin there was no problem there. But
what about a sarcophagus?

As they thought about this someone remembered that
stored away and forgotten at Windsor Castle was a massive
black marble sarcophagus that had lain unused for more
than 300 years.

The sarcophagus had originally been made for Cardinal
Wolsey. At the height of his power in 1521 Wolsey sent for
the Italian sculptor Rovezzano. He wanted a tomb in keeping

with his sense of his own worth. The vast sarcophagus that emerged from the hands of the Italian was extraordinarily impressive but before he had time to use it Wolsey fell out with Henry VIII. His palaces and houses were taken away and Wolsey was disgraced. Henry VIII decided that the black sarcophagus would be perfect for him so it was sent to Windsor to be ready when Henry died. When Henry finally gave up the ghost more than 20 years later, Rovezzano's magnificent work seems to have been overlooked, and it remained forgotten until those officials hunting around for something suitable for Nelson remembered the tomb's existence.

The really interesting question however is: how could something as big as Wolsey's sarcophagus have been forgotten and overlooked for so long?

THE MOLE
THAT KILLED A KING
1806

St James's Square retains just a few of its original early eighteenth-century houses, but this small square has been home at various times to an extraordinary list of the famous and the infamous – Gladstone and Pitt lived here along with half a dozen earls, several dukes and numerous royal mistresses. In fact within a decade of the square being built in 1670 every single house was lived in by someone who had a title or was sleeping with someone with a title.

But what makes the square really interesting is the bizarre statue of William III in the gardens. The statue is only here because the residents got fed up with the fact that the centre of the square was long used as a refuse tip for the householders – at one time it was piled high with 'kitchen rubbish, dead cats, scraps of timber and noxious mountains of refuse'. They wanted something to give the middle a purpose and a statue seemed as good an idea as anything. But that's where the problems began.

The idea of a statue of William was not initially popular so despite their enormous wealth the residents of the square refused to pay for it. Then a merchant offered money in his will but his family contested the will for the next 70 years and it wasn't until 1806 that the statue was finally completed.

Even when the statue was finally made and put on its plinth there was something odd about it – it includes, for example, a small molehill at the feet of the horse on which William is seated. What is the molehill for?

The answer is that William is said to have died after falling from his horse. The horse had tripped on a molehill.

William was the Protestant king brought to England from Holland to replace the last Catholic, King James II. James's supporters and all Jacobites then and now still toast the little gentleman in velvet – i.e. the mole that built the molehill that killed a king.

THE DIRTIEST PUB IN LONDON

1809

Many London pubs are far older than they might at first appear. In Bishopsgate, for example, Dirty Dicks dates back to the early eighteenth century despite the fact that the pub looks typically mid-Victorian. The cellars here are original and it was in the building above them that one of London's most extraordinary and eccentric characters once lived.

The story varies in its details but it seems that Richard, also known as Nathaniel, Bentley, a local businessman and dandy who ran a shop and warehouse, decided to get married. Everything was prepared and the dining room had been laid out with beautiful flowers, cutlery, linen and a huge cake, but on the night before the wedding his bride died. Distraught, Bentley sealed up the room where the table had been laid for the wedding breakfast and never opened it again. He also stopped washing and only changed his clothes when they rotted and fell off him.

He allowed his building to become one of the filthiest houses in London but people flocked to it to see if it really was as bad as they'd been told and Bentley made a fortune – a fortune he never spent because he bought nothing. He lived for nearly 40 years, and died finally in 1809. He was a rich man by then. He once said: 'What is the point of washing my hands or anything else for that matter when they will only be dirty again tomorrow?' The warehouse was later demolished.

The site was taken over by the Bishopsgate Distillery and the pub was known as The Old Jerusalem, but by the end of the nineteenth century the enterprising owner renamed the pub after its notorious resident, and the cellar bar displayed some of the less than hygienic relics from its past. Health and Safety have since ensured that these are confined to a display case near the toilets.

A MISTRESS'S REVENGE

1809

Disputes between lovers always involve emotional excesses and when lovers fall out it adds a new twist to the old saying: all's fair in love and war.

Salisbury Square, just off Fleet Street, once witnessed the conclusion to one of the strangest emotional disputes in the history of England. The problem began when Frederick, Duke of York (the second son of mad George III), began to lose interest in one of his mistresses, one Mrs Mary Anne Clarke. Mrs Clarke was his favourite mistress from 1803 until 1809 but then his enthusiasm began to wane. In short he completely lost interest in her. Mrs Clarke was furious at being unceremoniously dumped, but she would have accepted this meekly enough if the Duke had given her the pension she felt she deserved, together with a house in a fashionable part of London. The Duke for his part thought that he could simply discard her and that would be the end of it, but he had reckoned without the fury of a woman scorned.

When the Duke refused to see her or give her any money Mrs Clarke sat down and wrote her memoirs, in particular her memories of her relationship with the Duke. The notoriety of Mrs Clarke and the public's appetite for scandal meant the publisher was convinced he would have a huge sale and make his fortune, so he printed 10,000 copies – an enormous number for any book at the time. Mrs Clarke then let the Duke know that the book was about to come out. In earlier times he'd have had her head cut off, but even in Georgian England such an idea was unthinkable. The Duke knew when he was beaten. He immediately paid her a pension, bought her a house and bought up all 10,000 copies of the book – these were piled up in Salisbury Square and burned. If one copy survived and were to turn up now it would be worth a fortune!

NAPOLEON'S SOAP
ON SHOW
1816

It's hard to understand now, but despite the fact that he was defeated at Waterloo the Emperor Napoleon was one of the most popular figures in London at the beginning of the nineteenth century – popular in the sense that people were absolutely fascinated by everything to do with him now that he was safely imprisoned on the island of St Helena.

The great bogeyman of Europe who had terrified the British ruling classes (they thought he would encourage the lower orders to get above themselves) was now like a lion in a cage – awe-inspiring but harmless.

Napoleon fever reached a peak in around 1816 when the showman William Bullock bought a vast collection of Napoleon's personal effects – the collection included Napoleon's carriage, his horses, his combs, brushes, wine, spirits and even a small bar of his soap!

Even more extraordinary was the fact that Bullock managed to persuade Napoleon's former carriage driver to accompany the collection. It was all brought to Bullock's new British Museum, which was situated in Piccadilly, and within a few months almost half a million people had queued to see the collection. Bullock made a fortune and the British appetite for sensation was satisfied.

In fact Bullock did so well that he moved his collection of Napoleon artifacts into what he called the Museum Napoleon. But the obsession with the fallen Emperor didn't end there – a 431 sq. ft (40m^2) replica of the battlefield at Waterloo was created at the Egyptian Hall in Piccadilly with every detail, soldiers, artillery, horses and landmarks included.

HOW TO STOP
DEAD CATS FLYING

1819

One of the delights of London is that if you know what you
are looking for you will find odd, quirky little places in the
busiest thoroughfares and many of these have fascinating
and often curious histories. Piccadilly must be one of the
most famous streets in the world, but just off it is a row
of tiny Georgian shops virtually unchanged since they were
completed in 1819.

The shops in question are in the Burlington Arcade and
they are here for a most bizarre reason. Visitors often think
the Georgian planners who built these little shops were
simply building to make a profit. In fact they built the
arcade to cover a narrow alley that ran alongside Burlington
House, now the home of the Royal Academy but in the
early nineteenth century still a private home. The owner
of Burlington House was Lord George Cavendish, who had
complained for years that while sitting in his garden he was
constantly hit on the head by oyster shells, apple cores, old
bottles and even an occasional dead cat. These unpleasant
items were thrown over the wall between the garden and
the lane which then existed at its side. Cavendish decided
that a row of shops would put paid to the nuisance and so he
had them built and the alleyway vanished forever. Samuel
Ware was asked to design the beautiful shop fronts which
exist largely unchanged today, and though the shop interiors
are tiny the shopkeepers have always sold luxury goods, so

what they lack in quantity of stock they more than make up for in quality.

Originally the arcade was a single storey, but an upper level was added in 1906 and above the shops the rooms were let – according to one wag they were let to 'the better sort of courtesan'. The beautiful triple-arch entrance was destroyed for no good reason in 1931 and the new design was much hated. There was also some damage during the war but the arcade remains one of the world's first shopping malls. Instead of security men it still has a beadle who will ask you to leave the arcade if he catches you whistling, singing or humming (pimps used to whistle to their prostitutes as a warning that the police were nearby), running or carrying an open umbrella!

THE GREATEST LEGAL SCANDAL OF ALL

1819

The law has always been something of a scandalous institution. Lawyers have the best trade union in the sense that entry to the profession is strictly controlled and because lawyers never undercut each other and there is no genuine competition between practitioners, the poor public is always forced to pay very high prices for the advice it receives.

But the scandal of lawyers' costs today – a disgrace that no government dares tackle simply because politicians themselves tend to be drawn from the ranks of the legal profession – is nothing compared with the scandals of the past.

One of the greatest and most extraordinary of all legal humiliations, a scandal that outranks every other London legal dishonour, was known as the Great Jennings case.

Anyone who has read Charles Dickens's great novel of London life *Bleak House* will remember the case of Jarndyce and Jarndyce, which is the central symbol in that novel of social decay and corruption.

The case of Jarndyce and Jarndyce, though bizarre in its tortuousness, impenetrability and sheer longevity, was based on the Great Jennings case which was heard in the Old Hall, Lincoln's Inn. The real case was no less absurd than the story Dickens created to satirise it.

The Great Jennings case started in 1819 when Dickens

was only seven and didn't end until 1870, the year in which the great novelist died. But why was the case such a scandal? The answer is that the lawyers involved made no real efforts to conclude it; it was in their interest to keep it going as long as possible only because they were earning fat fees. The case finally ended when the money involved in the case ran out – it had all been used up funding lawyers' fees.

A CLUB FOR MEN
NOT ABLE TO SING
IN THE BATH

1820

Old pubs tend to survive longer than other buildings in London – with the exception of churches, of course. The Coal Hole in Carting Lane is a case in point. The present building dates back to the early 1800s but the pub commemorates an earlier nearby tavern of the same name.

The pub gets its name from the wharf used by coalmen that stood nearby before the Embankment pushed the river further away. For centuries coal was brought to London by ship from the mines of Northumberland and Durham (which is why in earlier centuries coal was always called sea coal) and the tough city coal heavers who lugged the sacks from the ships uphill to the carters liked to drink in this pub. During the eighteenth century the pub was hugely popular with actors and theatre managers including the great tragedian Edmund Kean (1787–1833), who started the Wolf Club.

The sole qualification for membership was that the applicant should have been forbidden by his wife to sing in the bath! The Wolf Bar in the present attractive Arts and Crafts interior with its pretty leaded windows commemorates this bizarre drinking club. And when you step out of the pub you can still look down the sloping lane and see the bright river – just as the coal heavers of earlier centuries did.

WOMEN BUYING MEN

1820

We are all familiar with the idea of men paying women for sex – prostitution is, after all, the world's oldest profession – but it is less common for the traffic to operate in the other direction. A bizarre tradition of women buying men did, however, exist in Victorian London though it probably only rarely led to sex.

The story begins with the bizarre development of Kensington Gardens and Hyde Park. To the modern visitor the two areas of open space seem almost indistinguishable, though they are divided by the road that crosses the park from Bayswater Road in the north to Kensington Gore in the south Kensington Gore takes its name from 'gara', an old English word describing a triangular plot of land which was left when ploughing fields of irregular shape.

Kensington Gardens really began to develop when William III decided he didn't like Whitehall Palace, the traditional home of English monarchs. He retreated to Kensington soon after 1688 and to the palace we see today. The gardens round the palace – including the famous Round Pond and the Broad Walk – were developed by Queen Anne and later by Queen Caroline, wife of George II.

It was Caroline who commissioned the work to dig the Serpentine – before Caroline, this had been a series of small ponds surrounded by marshland and through which the Westbourne River ran. When Caroline died George discovered that she'd stolen more than £26,000 of his money to complete the work. He was apparently furious as he'd been under the impression that the work had kept Caroline occupied for years and at no cost.

But throughout this period Kensington Gardens was a private area open only to royalty and their courtiers. Hyde Park by contrast was open to all and as a result it developed a slightly seedy reputation – prostitutes plied their trade here and robberies were commonplace.

By the beginning of the nineteenth century the rules were relaxed a little and Kensington Gardens was opened to 'the respectably dressed' – the gates were guarded by officials who turned away those who did not look respectable. At that time this meant the poor, who would have easily been identified by their practical, workday clothes.

But the ban on the lower orders meant that servant girls and soldiers from nearby Knightsbridge Barracks could not walk in the park. Instead they walked in Hyde Park and a tradition began that servant girls and others would pay soldiers to escort them – the girls wanted their friends to see them being escorted by a handsome guardsman in full dress uniform and they wanted it so badly they were prepared to pay for it.

A walk in the park with an artilleryman cost nine old pence; a guardsman's company for half an hour would set you back a shilling. If you could only afford a private it would cost sixpence. Such things would never have been allowed in Kensington Gardens.

But even until recently the distinction between the parks was very real and this was reflected in the way they were policed – until 2004 it was the Royal Parks Constabulary, funded by the Department for Culture, rather than the London Metropolitan Police that controlled the London Parks. Since 2004 the Royal Parks Operation Command Unit has been part of the Met.

TOM AND JERRY
IN LONDON

1821

If they think about them at all, most people probably imagine that the famous cartoon characters Tom and Jerry have their origin in the United States and more particularly in the vast film industry of that country.

In fact Tom and Jerry have their origins far earlier and on the other side of the Atlantic. The story starts in 1821 – well within the Georgian era – when London was enjoying a boom in publishing. Books, pamphlets and newspapers were being produced in ever greater numbers as literacy and the appetite for reading material spread through society.

A century earlier books had been largely the preserve of the rich or at least the comparatively well off, but by 1821 the popular press had taken off with a vengeance – in addition to cheap pamphlets and books there were broadsides (single news sheets usually about murders and executions), song sheets, chapbooks and penny dreadfuls.

Among the most innovative of the new publishers was Pierce Egan (1772–1849), a sporting journalist, who began a new series of publications in 1821 entitled *Life in London or the Day and Night Scenes of Jerry Hawthorne Esq and his elegant friend Corinthian Tom, accompanied by Bob Logic, the Oxonian, in their Rambles and Sprees Through the Metropolis*.

The series was so popular that other publishers produced pirated versions of it and within a few months it had been turned into a stage play – the title had changed by now to *Tom and Jerry or Life in London* but it was so popular and tripped so easily off the tongue that it is not difficult to see how it crossed the Atlantic in the head of some entrepreneur emigré and ended up transformed into the cartoon we know today. The basic idea of two characters getting into a series of scrapes remains the same but Egan's loveable human rogues have been transformed, of course, into a cat and a mouse.

WHEN THE DEAD MOVED
OUT OF LONDON

1832

Most visitors brave enough to include a graveyard on their
London itinerary go to Highgate cemetery to the north of
the city, but tucked away by the side of the Grand Union
Canal over to the west in what was until recently a fairly
poor part of North Kensington, Kensal Green Cemetery is
an extraordinary monument to Victorian funeral piety – and
even more bizarre funeral rituals.

Until the coming of the canal in the eighteenth century this
was a quiet place: there were a few houses at the junction
of Harrow Road and Kilburn Lane but the rest was open
farmland with an odd isolated inn and London half a day's
walk away. But by the early 1800s the small village centred
round the junction and its green was expanding. By the
1830s London's church graveyards were filled to bursting
and All Soul's Cemetery, as Kensal Green Cemetery was
originally known (the land was owned by All Souls College,
Oxford), was opened in 1832 to ease the problem.

Within a few years Kensal Rise Cemetery – as it quickly
became known – was the fashionable place to be buried.
Among the bizarre monuments the cemetery contains are
Greek temples, Egyptian halls, gothic fantasies and medieval
castles, as well as more ordinary but equally fascinating
gravestones and tombs. The cemetery is full of mature trees
and shrubs and gives every indication of being deep in the
heart of the countryside – among the tombs to look out for are

those of Sir Anthony Panizzi (1797–1879), who created the famous round Reading Room at the British Library (now part of the British Museum), Charles Babbage (1791–1871) who created the first computer, authors Wilkie Collins (1824–89), William Makepeace Thackeray (1811–63) and Anthony Trollope (1815–82), as well as the greatest of all the Victorian engineers, Isambard Kingdom Brunel (1806–59).

But Kensal Rise Cemetery has a strange secret – here and there are tombs that reveal an astonishing obsession that gripped Victorian Londoners for several decades. And what was this obsession? It was the fear of being buried alive.

From roughly 1870 until 1900 an idea grew up that doctors were constantly making mistakes when it came to deciding when a person had died. It was said that in many cases death certificates had been issued and the body was being prepared for laying out, when suddenly an eye flickered or the apparent corpse groaned. If a corpse could come back to life at this stage, who was to say that dozens – perhaps hundreds – had not been buried and only then come back to life?

Visitors to Highgate and Kensal Green cemeteries in London even today may see the remnants of a strange invention designed to guard against the risk of being buried on Monday and waking up in one's coffin on Wednesday. A number of tombs were built with a hollow stone column running down into the buried coffin. At the top of the hollow column 2–3ft (60–90cm) up in the air above the tombstone would be a small bell tower complete with bell.

The idea of the bizarre contraption was that if the deceased happened to wake up after burial he or she would be able to pull vigorously on a chain that ran up the hollow column to the bell, which would ring out, bringing rescuers hotfooting it across the fields.

A number of different coffin alarm systems were created around this time and, indeed, from then until well into the twentieth century, when in a few cases nervous relatives had electric alarms fitted to their relatives' coffins.

Despite all the terror and fears, however, there is no record of anyone buried with an alarm pressing the button or ringing the bell.

THE MAN WHO HAD HIMSELF STUFFED

1832

In earlier epochs the belief in the resurrection of the body – central to Christianity – meant that cremation was frowned on as a means of disposing of the dead. By the eighteenth century, in England at least, such ideas were being questioned and among the rationalists of the Enlightenment arguments about cremation versus burial came to seem absurd. It may well have been partly why the philosopher Jeremy Bentham (1748–1832), one of the great political and social thinkers of the later eighteenth and early nineteenth centuries, came up with a rather more unusual way of disposing of his own corpse.

Bentham's more than 60 published works cover everything from the need for political reform to animal welfare, discussions of the state of the colonies and the evils of swearing. Most famously, of course, he is associated with the creation of utilitarianism – the doctrine of the greatest good of the greatest number. He was also closely involved in the whole idea of a dissenters' university, which is what the University of London originally was. Dissenters were not allowed to study at the old universities so they set up their own. Bentham was considered wildly eccentric in his day for advocating universal suffrage and the decriminalisation of homosexuality.

The University of London started life in 1828 when Bentham was in his eighties and though he took no practical part in establishing it he is often considered its spiritual father, largely because of his advocacy of religious tolerance and education for all. Bentham loved the new university so it should come as no surprise that he left the university (later to become University College London) all his manuscripts. But he also left a legacy of surpassing eccentricity. Visitors to the South Cloisters of the main building cannot fail to see the large wooden and glass cabinet that stands in the corridor.

Inside the cabinet is a surprisingly lifelike and life-size Jeremy Bentham, comfortably seated with a stick in his hand and dressed in the very clothes he wore in life. The figure is not a model but the actual preserved remains of the great man. It was Bentham's last joke, if you like, at the expense of those who argued over burial and cremation for superstitious (i.e. religious) reasons.

When Bentham first arrived in his case a few weeks after his death in 1832, the head and face were actually those of Bentham, but the embalming technique used wasn't up to scratch and the head deteriorated badly until a wax replica had to be made. Bentham had left his body to the college on condition that it was preserved in this way and beneath the clothing even today Bentham's skeleton keeps an eye on the academic world he so loved in life.

Legends and extraordinary stories about the preserved philosopher abound – one says that he is wheeled into every university council meeting. At the end of each meeting the minutes record: Jeremy Bentham – present but not voting. Another legend has it that for a decade before he died Bentham carried around the glass eyes he wanted used in his preserved head. When they were finally used in the preserved head they fell out; then the head itself fell off and was found between Bentham's feet. Whatever the truth or otherwise of these and many other stories (including the one about the students found playing football with the head) we do know that in fact the real head is kept in the college vaults.

No one knows precisely why Bentham stipulated in his will that he should be preserved and set up for public display in this way, but it ties in nicely with the philosophy of a man who took a practical view of affairs and who thought it was important to make a contribution to the day-to-day life of the society in which he lived – at the end of his life he probably thought it would be nice to be in some position where he could watch the world go by and it was good to cock a snook at the more religious among his colleagues who were outraged at this refusal to stick to the Christian rules about the dead. No doubt Bentham also thought that if there was anything in the stories about the survival of the soul then his could hover where it had been happiest – in the corridors of the university.

IMMORAL BATHS

1835

When London's Charing Cross Hotel opened in the first half of the nineteenth century church leaders were outraged. The problem wasn't that it had built-in brothels or that it sold sex aids or rubber wear; no, the problem was far worse – the Charing Cross Hotel had too many bathrooms.

At a time when even the biggest hotel would have had at most half a dozen bathrooms the Charing Cross Hotel had almost one bathroom for every two bedrooms and the bishops assumed that if hotel guests were that keen to be clean it must be because they hoped to go bed hopping morning noon and night.

The bishops in the House of Lords denounced the owners of the hotel as little more than pimps.

WHY THE NATIONAL GALLERY HAS GIANT PEPPERPOTS

1835

When the National Gallery was built the architect found himself in a tricky position. His brief was to build something long and very narrow, as the access road behind the site (which is still there today) had to remain as it was when the royal stables, or mews, was here.

Not only that but, in a typically English and eccentric fudge, he also had to agree to build his new gallery no higher than the mews buildings it replaced. The idea was that the skyline at this point should look pretty much as it had done since the Middle Ages when the Royal Mews, a little to the north of the Palace of Westminster, was first established. The mews was where the king's animals – particularly his falcons – were 'mewed up'.

The architect of the National Gallery, as good as his word, came up with the design we see today and the oddest echo of the building the gallery replaced can be seen at either end of the present building. If you look carefully at the roof there are what look like two stone pepperpots, one at either end of the structure.

The reason these are here is that the original stables had almost identical decorative pepperpots – the originals were actually part of the ventilation system for the stables. As the heat and smell of the dung of several hundred horses rose it had to be dispersed from the building as quickly as possible – the pepperpots with their open stone latticework allowed just that to happen and the replacement pepperpots on the building have the same open decorative latticework, despite the fact that the horses departed forever nearly two centuries ago.

WORLD'S SMALLEST PRISON

1835

At one time most English towns and villages had lock-ups – small single-celled buildings where local drunks might be kept secure for the night or, where thieves or other antisocial individuals could be kept to await the arrival of the magistrate.

At the southeast corner of Trafalgar Square and missed by almost every tourist who comes to this place is a lock-up that is unique even by the standards of these odd little prisons, because the Trafalgar Square lock-up is also Britain's (possibly the world's) smallest police station.

The structure looks like a rather fat lamppost and it is only when one looks closely that one notices the tiny door and window. There is barely room for two people to stand upright inside but it is said that this tiny lock-up had and still has a direct telephone link to Scotland Yard.

Right up until the 1960s the Trafalgar Square lock-up was still in use, but it is by no means the only strange thing about this part of London. Take the famous lions at the bottom of Nelson's Column, for example. When the column was being built an artist had to be found to design the four huge lions round the base of the column. They are so much bigger than life size that it was feared the final result would be embarrassingly out of proportion unless someone with the right talents was chosen to complete the work.

Queen Victoria wanted Edwin Landseer (1862–73), one of

her favourite painters, to carry out the work but Landseer was horrified at the suggestion. He was not a sculptor and had no useful experience to bring to bear. He refused the commission, but the Queen would not give up. After being approached by peers and MPs, Landseer finally agreed but only on condition that he could take as long as he needed and that a dead lion would be sent round to his studio so he could study it before putting pen to paper.

It took several months before a lion died (presumably of natural causes) at London Zoo. It was immediately sent round to Landseer's house where he kept it until it stank so badly the neighbours began to complain. It took more than a year of preparatory drawing (and several more dead lions) before Landseer was finally happy – and the result was the splendid lions we see today.

But a century and more ago nothing seemed quite so straightforward – the drawings were ready but the sculpted lions were not installed until 25 years after they should have been put up. When Landseer died wreaths were draped around the lions' necks as a mark of respect.

Another curious tale concerns the capital at the top of the column on which Nelson's statue stands and the bronze bas-reliefs at the bottom of the column showing Nelson's victories (as well as his yet more famous death). All are made from French cannons captured after the Battle of Trafalgar in 1805.

THE TRAIN DISGUISED
AS A SHIP

1836

The train was to the nineteenth century what the Internet is to our century – the greatest scientific innovation of the age. It transformed Britain from a land of remote villages where people rarely travelled more than a few miles in all their lives to a place where eventually even the relatively poor could afford to travel distances undreamed of by their parents and grandparents.

The huge success of the very earliest railways in the north of England meant that trains quickly spread and, of course, part of the spread took the iron roadway to London. The earliest London service of all was that which ran from the City to Greenwich.

Crowds gathered in those early days to see the extraordinary new invention – a breathing monster that could pull huge loads without the assistance of horses. The new method of transport was very popular with the travelling public, or at least that part of it wealthy enough to indulge in what was seen as a luxury, but much as people admired the technology there were many complaints about the aesthetics of the whole enterprise. The chief complaint was that somehow the engines were rather ugly. Letters were written in great numbers to the railway company asking if they could not brighten up these dismal-looking locomotives. The real problem was that the first generation to experience railways judged them against the brightly coloured mail coaches that still dominated the national transportation system. Since coaches were still on the scene, though declining in numbers, older people looked back to them through the rose-tinted spectacles of nostalgia and hoped that the rather brash trains could be somehow given the glamour and glitter of the older form of transportation.

According to the then editor of the Railway News, the London and Greenwich Railway (L&GR) company took the complaints about the appearance of their engines very seriously. They studied the problem and after some time one of their engineers came up with a solution. Because the brick-built viaducts that carried the line into London looked rather like Roman aqueducts an eccentric engineer at the L&GR suggested to Braithwaite and Milner, who made the company's engines, that they should build a locomotive in the style of a Roman galley!

The result was that a year later huge crowds gathered at Cornhill in the City to watch the arrival of a long line of carriages pulled by a very passable imitation of an ancient ship. When word got out much of the route was regularly lined with spectators eager to see this extraordinary engine, which was – as its inventor had suggested – particularly impressive when viewed from the ground as it passed sedately over one or other of the company's viaducts.

The only thing that spoiled the general effect was the noise and the clouds of dense smoke.

Despite its initial popularity the idea of locomotives imitating ships did not catch on and the London and Greenwich soon reverted to more practical-looking engines.

TRAFALGAR SQUARE – PERMANENTLY UNFINISHED

1838

Present-day Trafalgar Square is built on the site where Henry VIII and earlier kings once kept their birds of prey and their horses. The site was first built on when Chaucer was Clerk of the King's Works in the 1380s and Richard II needed somewhere close to the rambling Palace of Whitehall for the royal hawks. Gradually the word mews was used not just for hawks and falcons but for other animals kept either for royal use or entertainment.

The royal mews lasted well beyond the destruction by fire of the Palace of Westminster but the area in which the mews stood gradually became a warren of small dirty lanes where 'thieves and vagabonds abound', but by the time the area (by then known as the Bermudas) was cleared completely to allow for the building of the present square the word 'mews' had passed into the language and meant any narrow alleyway where horses were kept. Today in Belgravia and Mayfair the narrow back lanes behind grand house are still often called mews, for here the servants lived in small cottages or above the stables where their employers' horses were kept.

Like most building projects in London, Trafalgar Square was the subject of endless disputes and arguments – the plans for the National Gallery (completed in 1838) were derided by many who thought the proposed building an architectural disaster.

But unlike most projects, which are eventually built and completed, however greatly modified during the planning process, Trafalgar Square has never been completed and remains unfinished to this day.

The unfinished bit is the empty plinth in the northwest corner – this has been empty ever since the square was first built and though in recent years some bizarre sculptures have been placed on the unused plinth (including an upside-down, see-through version of the plinth itself!) there are still no plans to erect a permanent statue here.

THE MYSTERIOUS
CROSSING SWEEPER
1840

It's easy to forget that London's streets were, until comparatively recently, completely uncared for. In Victorian times many streets were cobbled, or were made from wooden sets (blocks of wood packed tightly with their end-grain uppermost to reduce wear) but elsewhere they were entirely unmade. In poorer districts the population would still throw their slops into the street just as their medieval ancestors did. And of course everywhere was the dung left by thousands of horses. But the mess in the streets had one great advantage – it produced jobs for hundreds if not thousands of London's poorest citizens. These were the crossing sweepers. Perhaps the most famous crossing sweeper – a trade that vanished with the coming of the motor car – was Jo in Charles Dickens's novel *Bleak House*. Jo was Dickens's attempt to show how damaging it was to society as a whole to allow children to live the sort of life Jo lives. Illiterate, half-dressed even in winter and forced to sleep in the streets, Jo earns a few pennies each day by sweeping a path through the horse manure from one side of a London street to another. Many destitute men, women and children were forced to do this work simply because they had nothing else, but one of the most remarkable stories of a crossing sweeper concerns a real-life sweeper called Brutus Billy or Charles McGhee.

Nothing is known of McGhee's history, but he was an

elderly black man who had probably come to England from the West Indies.

For many years in the early nineteenth century he swept a path across Fleet Street where it meets Ludgate Hill near a wealthy linen draper's shop in Fleet Street. The shop was owned by Robert Waithman who later became MP for the City of London. From the window above the shop the draper's daughter watched the old crossing sweeper and on cold days she arranged for someone to take him a bowl of hot soup and some bread. When McGhee died some years later it was discovered that he had left all his savings – some £700, which was an extraordinary sum in Victorian times – to the draper's daughter.

A BRIDGE FROM
LONDON TO BRISTOL

1845

The Clifton Suspension Bridge is one of the wonders of nineteenth-century engineering, but one of the strangest things about it – a fact that is almost forgotten today – is that it started life in central London.

The story begins with the decision by the Earl of Hungerford to build a fruit and vegetable market to rival the one at Covent Garden. Hungerford market began life in 1692 on the site now occupied by Charing Cross Station but it never came to rival Covent Garden, the more famous market down the road. An attempt to improve things – by bringing customers in from south of the river – came when Isambard Kingdom Brunel built Hungerford Suspension Bridge in 1845.

Hungerford market finally disappeared when the railway company bought the land and built Charing Cross Station, but they too needed a bridge over the river and it would have to carry trains.

Before the current walkways were built, the railway company sold the old suspension bridge to the city of Bristol and then built their new railway bridge – in the strict legal sense there are still two bridges here, which may explain why on some maps the existing bridge is referred to as Hungerford Bridge while others insist on calling it Charing Cross Bridge. The reason is that the London public had got used to being able to cross the bridge and the railway company's plan would have deprived them of their old crossing because the new bridge would have been used by trains only. The railway company was forced by public pressure to build its railway bridge with a pedestrian footbridge alongside, which is why today the railway bridge into Charing Cross Station is the only railway bridge in London that also has a pedestrian footbridge. The pedestrian footbridge is Hungerford Bridge, while the railway bridge alongside is Charing Cross Bridge.

WHY BIG BEN ISN'T
BIG BEN AT ALL
1852

Big Ben is one of London's oddest buildings and the story of how it came to be built is typical of the eccentric way in which things tend to get done in London. Like the rest of the Palace of Westminster, it was built by Charles Barry (1795–1860) and Augustus Pugin (1812–52) after a nationwide competition to find a new design for the seat of government after the disastrous fire of 1834.

The late Georgian passion for Gothic gave the Barry design a head start and after duly winning the competition, he began building the clock tower we see today, but when it was first built it wasn't known as Big Ben at all – the name Big Ben refers to the huge bell on which the hours are struck.

All the statistics to do with St Stephen's Tower (renamed the Elizabeth Tower to commemorate the Queen's Diamond Jubilee in 2012) – as Big Ben is really known – and its great clock are astonishing: the tower is nearly 320ft (98m) high; and it took almost 19 years from laying the first foundation stone to getting the clock going, largely because no one could agree about who should make it.

The job was first offered to Benjamin Vulliamy, the Queen's clockmaker, who was based in Pall Mall. His design was attacked as absurd and incompetent by another clockmaker, J. Dent, and after a huge fight with letters banging to and fro and *Times* leaders thundering out various opinions, the commissioners charged with organising the work gave in and launched a competition to design and build the new clock.

The contract finally went to Dent amid much acrimony, in 1852. Two years later the unique clock – 15½ft (4.7m) long by nearly 5ft (1.5m) wide – was ready, but there was nowhere to put it because wrangles over the building of the tower had delayed construction.

While all this was being sorted out, an east London company cast a great 16-ton bell, but during tests using a 13-hundredweight (660kg) clapper the bell cracked. It then had to be melted down and recast, this time by the Whitechapel Bell foundry. It took 16 horses the best part of a day to haul the gigantic bell to Parliament Square. It was then hoisted into position at the top of the tower, which was completed just in time.

When the clock began to run it was discovered that the 2½-ton hands were so heavy that the mechanism could not move them. They were redesigned in a lighter metal but now crashed down past the three each time they reached 12. Remade for a third time in hollow copper, they worked and they have kept time accurately ever since.

There are two theories about the origins of the name 'Big Ben': around the time the clock was due to be completed, the prizefighter and publican Ben Caunt went 60 rounds with the best bare-knuckle boxer in the country, Nat Langham. The bout was declared a draw but it made both men national heroes. Ben Caunt was a huge man and one story has it that the great bell was named after him. The other story attributes the name to Benjamin Hall, the chief commissioner of works, who was addressing the House on the subject of a name for the new bell tower when, to great laughter, someone shouted 'Call it Big Ben!'

Perhaps the most remarkable thing about the clock is that even by the standards of today's atomic timepieces it is wonderfully accurate. When the commissioners launched their competition to design it they stipulated that it must be accurate to within one second an hour – most clock makers at the time agreed that this was impossible but that's how accurate the clock still is today. If it does get slightly out of time, penny coins used as necessary, kept especially for the purpose, are placed on the huge pendulum and the weight of the coin or coins is enough to adjust the clock by a fraction of a second.

TRAINS ONLY
FOR THE DEAD
1854

Just outside Waterloo Station between what was once York Street (it was recently renamed Leake Street) and the Westminster Bridge Road is a curious reddish building with a grey-stone arched entranceway. This is the former entrance to one of London's most extraordinary railway stations.

The current building dates from the early twentieth century but it replaced a station building opened on the same site in 1854. The station was the London terminus for the Necropolis Railway – a railway devoted entirely to the dead.

To find out how this bizarre situation came about we have to remember that by the mid-nineteenth century London's churchyards were full to overflowing. Bodies were stamped down into graves already too full and in many cases just a few inches of soil covered the decaying corpses. The result was appallingly insanitary conditions and frequent outbreaks of disease.

To ease the problems London's churchyards were closed and building began on a number of out-of-town cemeteries – Kensal Green and, more famously, Highgate. South of London, Brookwood Cemetery was opened some 25 miles (40.2km) from London, but the great difficulty was how to get corpse, coffin and mourners there. The solution was the Necropolis Railway.

Funeral trains ran from what was really a private station attached to the main line. Once out of the station the funeral trains joined the main line until they reached Brookwood. Here they reversed into the grounds of the cemetery. Until 1902 when the station was rebuilt following the complete rebuilding of the rest of Waterloo Station, Necropolis trains ran every day if there was a booking. After 1900, for some inexplicable reason, trains ceased to run on Sundays and a few years later they were running no more than twice a week. In 1941 the station was bombed (the façade survived) and the funeral trains were never revived after the war.

In the late 1940s the track from London to Brookwood was taken up but the station and track survived in the grounds of Brookwood Cemetery for a little longer. There were two stations in the cemetery – the north station served Nonconformists and the south station served the Anglican dead. The north station was demolished in the early 1960s but the south station survived until a fire in 1972. Today, the remains of the station platforms can still be seen at Brookwood – the only reminder of the thousands of dead who took their last journey on the Necropolis railway.

FREE LOVE IN VICTORIAN CLAPTON

1859

In the first centuries of the Christian era there were dozens if not hundreds of odd little sects and heretical groups that broke away from the ancient Jewish tradition (as did Jesus himself) and claimed that their leader was the messiah. 'Christos' is merely the Greek rendering of the Hebrew word 'messiah'.

Many of these early sects were ruthlessly suppressed as what was considered 'orthodox' belief came to be enforced by one particular group – the Christians. This, of course, later split into the Roman Catholic strand of Christianity and the Orthodox strand. But there were also many gnostic (meaning secret knowledge) Christian sects whose beliefs were considered heretical.

One gnostic sect believed that Judas was the one true disciple on the grounds that he was the only one who helped Christ slough off his mortal body. The existence of this gnostic strand of early Christianity was confirmed spectacularly when in 2004 scholars discovered a previously unknown gospel from the late third century – this was the Gospel of Judas Iscariot.

In later centuries, Christianity was split and riven by other sects, the Rosicrucians, Muggletonians, Ranters and Peculiar People among others. Most spectacular of all, of course, was the major split that occurred at the Reformation.

But a little church in north London which still stands

today was once home to a Christian sect that was bizarre even by the standards of early gnostic and other apocalyptic sects.

The church, whose architecture hardly betrays its bizarre origins, was once the home of the Agapemonites, a sect that – like the American Mormons – has its origins in one man's desire to legitimise a promiscuous sex life.

The story begins with Henry James Prince who, while a student at St David's theological college in Wales, set up the Lampeter Brethren in 1836. Ordained at the age of 28, Prince made himself head of the brethren whose main aim seems to have been what in the 1960s would have been termed free love. By 1859 Prince had married a wealthy woman who then conveniently died. He also resigned from the Church of England and set up the Agapemonites using money he'd inherited from his wife. Prince was apparently a remarkably charismatic man and within a few years his new church – 'agapemone' is Greek for 'abode of love' – was attracting numerous followers. Women seem to have been particularly keen to join. All new members pooled their wealth and lived communally under the rule of Prince.

A wealthy London businessman gave Prince a huge donation and agreed to become the great man's butler, but when Prince helped himself to Louisa Nottidge's fortune her family sued him and won – the Agapemonites had to pay the money back. Despite an occasional setback the Agapemonites were now wealthy enough to build the church that still stands in the Clapton district of Hackney. The building was known as the Ark of the Covenant and it cost £16,000 to build.

By the 1890s the church was attracting people from across the world, though in relatively small numbers. They came to listen to Prince tell them that he was John the Baptist come back to Earth. By the end of the century he was telling his congregation that he was no longer John the Baptist but had become the Incarnation of the Holy Ghost.

Prince's right-hand man was John Hugh Smyth Piggot, a parson who had studied at the London College of Divinity in Highbury. He met Prince in Ireland in the mid-1880s and was a member of the Salvation Army for a while.

The two men seemed to have spent most of their time persuading the female members of their congregation that the way to salvation was via the bedroom. But there was an occasional explanation of the sect's more general theological ideas – the Testimony, for example, was published in the 1890s. It is astonishing it ever convinced anyone given that it is full of precisely the same sort of predictions and pronouncements that characterise pretty much every other oddball sect from the Mormons to the Jehovah's Witnesses.

The Testimony says that the world is about to end and that members of the church must be celibate unless called upon by the church itself to sacrifice their celibacy in pursuit of a higher truth. Prince insisted that as the Lord's anointed he must travel in style – he had a coach and four and whenever he thundered through the London streets his coach was accompanied by a full complement of foxhounds.

He told his followers that as a spirit he could not die so it must have come as a shock when he dropped dead in 1899.

What really astonished his followers, however, was the fact that Prince had condemned every other church member who had died – he had said that any member who died only did so because he had not lived properly according to the rules of the Agapemonites. As he, by implication, was supremely aware of how a good Agapemonite should live he would never die, but die he did.

Prince was buried upright (another Agapemonite idea) and Piggot took over as leader. Piggot clearly thought that Prince had undersold himself when he declared that he was John the Baptist (and later the Holy Ghost) so on 7 September 1902 he told his congregation something even more remarkable. His exact words were recorded for posterity:

Christ suffered for sin and it was promised for them that waited for him He would appear a second time with salvation to man from death and judgement. Brother Prince was sent before his Lord's face to prepare the way for the second coming of him who suffered for sin, to prepare the way for the restoration of all things.

His testimony was true and the word of the holy ghost in him was perfect and I who speak to you tonight – I am that Lord Jesus Christ who died and rose again and ascended into heaven. I am that Lord Jesus Christ come again in my own body to save those who come to me from death and judgment.

Yes, I am he that liveth and behold I am alive for ever more. I am come again for the second time as the bridegroom of the church and the judge of all men, for the father has committed all judgment unto me because I am the son of man. And you – each one of you – must be judged by me.

By the following Sunday word of this astonishing sermon had leaked out and a crowd of more than 6,000 gathered outside the Ark of the Covenant. Police were called to keep order and the mood grew ugly. In earlier times, of course, anyone claiming to be Jesus would have been burned at the stake. The Edwardians of north London were cross but not that cross – they confined themselves to jeering Piggot when he arrived in his coach and four.

In the event the police failed to keep order and the crowd surged into the church, where Piggot duly repeated his claim to be Jesus.

Piggot's coach was bombarded with sticks, stones and bricks as he travelled home and such was the scandal surrounding his outrageous claims that the sect was forced to move to a remote location in Somerset. Here a young woman called Ruth Preece joined the sect and became Piggot's second wife.

Life was strict in the Somerset Abode of Love – the women members of the sect were known as helps (they did all the work) who might graduate to be ornamentals, entitled to be waited on by the helps. About 30 of the youngest and most attractive members of the sect became Piggot's concubines. Piggot sat on a gilded throne and everyone had to call him master.

Ruth Preece eventually became spiritual bride in chief but seems to have got on well with the first Mrs Piggot.

In 1909 it became known to the church authorities that Piggot's concubines had given birth and a consistory court was instituted to try Piggot in absentia. He was defrocked on 9 March.

By this time more than 100 women were living at the Abode of Love with Piggot. As he grew older all sorts of potions were tried in an attempt to keep him young and vigorous; all failed. He died in 1927 and the sect was taken over by Douglas Hamilton. The sect began to decline and by the 1940s only a dozen or so members were left. Piggot's two sons served in the forces; his daughter vanished abroad. Hamilton died in 1942.

By 1950 the tiny group of remaining sect members were still convinced that Piggot would return to them. He did not and the last of the Agapemonites – Ruth Preece – survived into the 1960s. The Ark of the Covenant in Clapton still stands but is now a Catholic church. Piggot's bizarre sect has gone forever.

MR CRAPPER'S BOTTOM
SLAPPER

1860

A strange London story that turns out not to be true is that
the word 'crap' – in the vulgar lavatorial sense – comes
from the pioneer of the flushing lavatory, Thomas Crapper
(1837–1910). But even if that is not true there remain some
wonderful tales about Crapper, who walked penniless to
London in 1850 aged 14, and became apprenticed to a
master plumber in Chelsea. A decade later he had set up
on his own and his company soon became the most famous
sanitary-ware manufacturer in the world – a manufacturer
that was still in existence in the early 1960s.

Crapper was a brilliant engineer who revolutionised the
way we go to the loo. Before Crapper, London lavatories
relied on turning a simple tap on to flush the loo, but the
problem with this system was that people forgot to turn the
tap off and water was left running (sometimes intentionally)
all the time. A trickle of water did not make for a particularly
hygienic flushing system. The result was a chronic loss of
pressure in London's water system and badly flushing loos.

Crapper's flushing lavatory was brilliant because it was
automatic, saved water and was propelled by enough force
to flush properly. Instead of the loo with a simple running
tap he invented the system we use today – a small tank
filled automatically with no risk of overflow and using only
relatively small amounts of water. The tank also produced
enough pressure to flush the loo properly in one go.

So convinced was he of the brilliance of his various designs that he invited a bemused public into the works every now and then to see how a particular loo and cistern combination could flush away a dozen apples or several potatoes. Visits became one of the highlights of Saturday afternoons in Chelsea!

Crapper also invented the disconnecting trap – a device fitted in each soil pipe just below ground that prevented the smell of the drains coming back up into the house.

Crapper seems to have been almost the only Victorian not to have been squeamish and permanently embarrassed by matters lavatorial, but on one famous occasion in the early days of his success he put his loos and cisterns in the window of his shop in Chelsea and several lady passers-by fainted with shock!

Not all Crapper's inventions were warmly greeted, however. He invented a loo that used a complicated system of pistons attached to the loo seat to flush the loo automatically. Having used the loo the user stood up and the loo seat automatically rose up – the rising movement automatically activating the flushing mechanism. However, it was discovered that within a few months of being fitted the loo seat began to stick – this meant that the unsuspecting user would begin to stand up only to find that the loo seat stuck until enough pressure had built up from the system to unstick it. The loo seat would then fly up at speed, hitting the user painfully on the bottom. The invention became known as the bottom slapper and was eventually discontinued.

Thomas Crapper died in 1910 but the firm he founded was still being run by his descendants in 1963, when it was finally sold to a rival company. Crapper was never honoured despite the fact that his flushing loo probably did far more to improve the health and happiness of humans worldwide than any number of politicians, businessmen, army generals and celebrities put together.

HOW TO MAKE A LIVING SELLING DOG POO

1861

Poverty in earlier centuries pushed tens of thousands of Londoners into very peculiar occupations – peculiar at least by modern standards. There was a huge market for live birds, for example, and this market was met by hundreds of live-bird sellers who might walk 20 miles (32km) out of London to catch a dozen or so birds before walking the 20 miles back again. They would then repeat this journey three or four times a week.

Or take the mudlarks who scoured the river foreshore at low tide. They went barefoot whatever the weather, searching for copper nails from the ships, for old bottles – anything in fact that they might be able to sell.

The toshers, on the other hand, were men who risked their lives searching for valuables in London's vast, unmapped warren of sewers. Toshers tended to be from the same few families and they handed down their knowledge of the sewer network from generation to generation, but even generations of experience couldn't always protect them and many died when sudden rainfall flooded the system or the lamps and candles they carried were blown out or they were overcome by gas.

But perhaps the strangest job of all was that of the pure finder – a job that existed, perhaps could only have existed, in Victorian London.

A pure finder was someone who spent his days searching

for dog faeces to sell to leather tanners, particularly to those tanners engaged in producing leather for the bookbinding trade.

Henry Mayhew's extraordinary book *London Labour and the London Poor* charts the lives of a number of pure finders. Mayhew explains that in the 1830s and 1840s groups of old women specialised in collecting used rags and were known as 'bunters'; later they added the collection of pure to their original job description. By the 1850s, when Mayhew carried out his research, men, women and children were working as pure finders. Pure finders sold the dog faeces they collected for roughly ten old pence a bucketful. The tanners – mostly based in Bermondsey (where 30 tanneries are recorded in the 1860s) – preferred the dry sort of faeces as it contained more alkaline and it was the alkaline that worked its magic on the leather.

Curiously, Mayhew and others recorded that many of the pure finders were well-educated men and women who had fallen on hard times. His description is hugely evocative:

The pure-finder is often found in the open streets, as dogs wander where they like. The pure-finders always carry a handle basket, generally with a cover, to hide the contents, and have their right hand covered with a black leather glove; many of them, however, dispense with the glove, as they say it is much easier to wash their hands than to keep the glove fit for use. The women generally have a large pocket for the reception of such rags as they may chance to fall in with, but they pick up those only of the very best quality, and will not go out of their way to search even for them. Thus equipped they may be seen pursuing their avocation in almost every street in and about London, excepting such streets as are now cleansed by the street orderlies, of whom the pure-finders grievously complain, as being an unwarrantable interference with the privileges of their class.

The pure collected is used by leather-dressers and tanners, and more especially by those engaged in the manufacture of morocco and kid leather from the skins of old and young goats, of which skins great numbers are imported, and of the roans and lambskins which are the sham morocco and kids of the slop leather trade, and are used by the better class of shoemakers, bookbinders, and glovers, for the inferior requirements of their business. Pure is also used by tanners, as is pigeons' dung, for the tanning of the thinner kinds of leather, such as calf-skins, for which purpose it is placed in pits with an admixture of lime and bark.

In the manufacture of moroccos and roans the pure is rubbed by the hands of the workman into the skin he is dressing. This is done to purify the leather, I was told by an intelligent leatherdresser, and from that term the word pure has originated. The dung has astringent as well as highly alkaline, or, to use the expression of my informant, scouring, qualities. When the pure has been rubbed into the flesh and grain of the skin (the flesh being originally the interior, and the grain the exterior part of the cuticle), and the skin, thus purified, has been hung up to be dried, the dung removes, as it were, all such moisture as, if allowed to remain, would tend to make the leather unsound or imperfectly dressed. This imperfect dressing, moreover, gives a disagreeable smell to the leather and leather-buyers often use both nose and tongue in making their purchases ...

WHERE IS THE CENTRE OF LONDON?

1865

One of the oddest things about London is that most people have no idea where it begins – or more precisely where its centre actually is. Many think that the statue of Eros in Piccadilly Circus marks the centre point; others are convinced that Buckingham Palace marks the spot, or St Paul's Cathedral.

In fact – and for the strangest reason – the centre of London is located at a spot just behind the equestrian statue of Charles I at the southern edge of Trafalgar Square. If you look carefully there is a brass plate in the roadway that marks the precise spot.

But what adds to the oddity of this is that strictly speaking – and despite modern rearrangements to suit the traffic – the brass plate set in the ground here is not in Trafalgar Square at all. It is Charing Cross. The Charing Cross we see today – which is outside the Charing Cross railway hotel just a few hundred yards away – was put up in 1865 as a publicity stunt to attract attention to the new railway terminus.

The medieval Charing Cross from which the area gets its name was actually at the top of Whitehall where the brass plaque is now.

But why choose this exact spot to define the centre of London? The answer has to do with the bizarre growth of the capital – to the east of the plaque is the City of London; to the south Westminster.

Edward the Confessor (1003–66) made a vow to go on a pilgrimage to Rome, but domestic unrest made this impossible and he sought absolution from his vow by promising to build a huge church. He chose Thorney Island for his church – a small area of high ground above the surrounding marsh of the Thames. This area – we now call it Westminster – already had a small monastery, but Edward enlarged it considerably and added Westminster Abbey, the church we see today. The new church was complete by 1065.

The merchants of the City had no intention of moving to what was then a windswept and remote location so they stayed put, but when the legislators at Westminster Hall wanted to hear news of the commercial goings on of the City they came to the halfway point – Charing Cross – and the City merchants wanting to know more of affairs of state also came to this spot.

The brass plaque marks the exact halfway point between the old city and the new seat of government and is therefore the centre point, as it were, of both Londons.

With the growth of the civil service in the nineteenth and twentieth centuries the brass plaque helped solve a more practical problem too: where London weighting was paid to public officials there had to be a decision about the area of London within which the extra rate of pay would be calculated. It was decided that anyone working within a 6-mile (9.7km) radius of the brass plaque at Charing Cross would be entitled to the extra payment.

THE HOUSES THAT EXIST
BUT AREN'T THERE
1868

An elegant stuccoed street in Paddington hides one of the oddest pairs of houses in the world. The passer-by would hardly notice that numbers 23 and 24 Leinster Gardens have permanently darkened windows, nor that the front doors have a curiously solid feel to them. But look closely and you quickly realise that these are not actually houses at all.

The story starts in the 1860s when the world's first underground railway was being constructed. The Metropolitan line – which was opened in 1868 – was built on the cut and cover principle. This meant that to build a tunnel you first had to dig a huge trench. Once this was done the circular supports (to make the tunnel) were fitted and the whole then covered with earth again. When the line between Bayswater and Paddington was being built it became necessary to demolish two houses in what was then a recently built and highly prestigious row of terraced houses.

Numerous railway acts tended to ride roughshod over the rights of tenants and landlords in the mid-Victorian era so the railway company simply compulsorily purchased two houses in the path of their tunnel and knocked them down. But the householders on either side refused to be beaten by a mere Act of Parliament – they managed to force through a condition that when the tunnel had been built and covered over, the façades at least of the two demolished houses should be reinstated. And that is precisely what happened. What look like a pair of rather grand houses are actually only walls about 5ft (1.5m) thick.

If you retrace your steps from Leinster Gardens to Porchester Road, which runs parallel to Leinster Gardens, you come to a long wall. Look over this and you will see the backs of 23 and 24 Leinster Gardens – a high, blank brick wall held up by steel girders. Below the wall is the tunnel entrance. But this is only a short stretch of exposed railway and it could have been covered over. The reason it is still open to the skies is that the first underground railway trains were steam driven and though they were specially adapted to reduce steam and smoke emissions in the tunnels (which would have been very unhealthy for passengers) they did have to release large amounts of coal exhaust fumes now and then. The spot behind the fake houses was established as an acceptable place for those early drivers to vent their engines!

ISLAMIC SEWAGE CENTRE
1868

Many of London's strangest tales concern buildings put up for the oddest reasons – either the fashion of the time or as a result of the eccentricity of architect or owner. But there are a number of buildings put up in odd styles to hide their real purpose.

The Abbey Mills pumping station is a good example. This dotty-looking building with its Moorish domes and towers, looks like something from Asia or the Middle East – in fact it was built in Victorian times (during a period of enthusiasm for all things Islamic) to disguise, of all things, a sewage works!

The interior is even more bizarre as it looks exactly like an Eastern Orthodox Church.

The architect was Joseph Bazalgette (1819–91), the man who rescued London from drowning in its own sewage by building the embankments along the Thames and their massive sewers that were designed to carry London's waste miles downstream and away from the bulk of the populace.

Balzalgette's embankment also provided a perfect place to build tunnels for the Circle and District lines as well – later on – as masses of communications wires and pipes.

The embankment sewer scheme had been proposed after Parliament found it increasingly difficult to meet at all in summer because of the stench from the river – at times it was so bad that huge sheets of canvas soaked in vinegar had to be hung behind the windows of the palace of Westminster. Without them the Parliamentarians were unable to stay in the chamber long enough to make any decisions. Bazalgette came up with the answer. But the embankment was only part of the solution and Bazalgette was given responsibility for the whole of London's main drainage system. Hence Abbey Mills pumping station.

Completed in 1868, it had to be made to look like something – anything – other than a sewage pumping station because the Victorians couldn't bear the idea of anyone going to the lavatory and would not have taken kindly to a large building clearly designed with sewage in mind. But with a Moorish palace in their midst they could kid themselves that it had nothing to do with bodily functions of any kind.

A ROAR ON THE
EMBANKMENT

1870

The Thames has always dominated life in London – the
City's huge wealth was built on trade via the river and for
centuries most people travelled across London by water as
the roads were almost always either cluttered or deep in
mud or both.

London was in constant danger of flooding too and even
today, with the Thames Barrier in place, rising sea levels
could threaten the city again.

The real problem with flooding when the embankment
walls were built was that, despite the great height of the
embankment walls, they had the effect of narrowing the
river and increasing its depth. Add to that the fact that
nothing could control the great surges that began far out at
sea and then drove remorselessly upriver. When heavy rain
in winter coincided with a big spring tide the embankment
was often breached in numerous places, causing tens of
thousands of pounds of damage to property, not to mention
disruption to transport and people's lives generally.

There was, however, a bizarre and rather primitive early
warning system that is still partially in use today.

Anyone who has ever leaned over the embankment to gaze
out along the river will probably have noticed that well below
the parapet and fixed at regular intervals into the stonework
there are lions' heads with mooring rings hanging from
their mouths. Visitors often wonder why on earth so many

mooring positions should be required so far below the top of the wall – the passengers of any boat tying up at any of these rings could not possibly disembark.

The solution to this mystery is tied up with the early warning system for flooding that existed in London before the Thames Barrier was built. Every policeman whose beat happens to take him along the embankment on either side of the river was formerly instructed to keep an eye on the lions' heads, because if the water level reaches the heads flooding is a serious and imminent danger. The rule used to be that once the water reached the heads all Underground stations were closed and London was put on red alert.

THE HOUSE WHERE TIME
STOOD STILL

1874

There is a common misconception that London is still a wonderful place to find eighteenth- and early nineteenth-century architecture despite the deadly work of redevelopers and German bombs, but actually the majority of eighteenth-century houses are only eighteenth century in outward appearance. Only a few rare examples are listed

in such a way as to prevent their interiors being destroyed, even if their façades have to be left unchanged. This means that thousands of modern houses and office blocks have eighteenth-century fronts. In the 1960s this even happened to houses of great architectural merit – like Schomberg House in Pall Mall, a beautiful seventeenth-century house that developers were allowed to destroy so long as they kept the façade. Great houses and churches often survive with their interiors but the least likely to survive of all are the interiors of the houses of the middle and working classes.

Linley Sambourne House is an extraordinary exception to that rule. Named after the cartoonist who lived here from 1874–1910, it is a perfect example of a solidly middle-class household of the mid-Victorian period. When Sambourne and his young wife moved into the house, which had been built only four years earlier, they decorated in the then fashionable aesthetic style – characterised by heavy velvet drapes, William Morris wallpapers, ornate Turkey carpets and a vast clutter of china ornaments.

Sambourne earned his living as a cartoonist, mostly for *Punch* magazine, for almost half a century. Most of his drawings were completed in this house and numerous examples of his work can be seen, along with his photographs – like many artists of the time he was fascinated by this still relatively new art form.

The house remained substantially unchanged through the twentieth century through extraordinary good luck. The Sambournes' son Roy inherited the house and left it unchanged, probably because he never married. When he in turn died he left the house to his elder sister Maud. She too was passionate about preserving it intact, largely because – as she said herself – she'd been so happy there as a child. Her daughter Anne then used the house until at a party in 1957 Anne proposed that she and her friends, including the future Poet Laureate John Betjeman (1906–84), should found the Victorian Society to preserve the house and its contents and to work for the preservation of other similar examples of Victorian taste. The Victorian style was then hugely unpopular – how unpopular can be judged by the fact that sometime in the mid-1950s Lord Leighton's famous painting 'Hope', now one of the most popular works in the collection of pictures at Tate Britain, was used to block up an old fireplace in a house in Battersea!

A NEEDLE BY THE RIVER

1878

Londoners have never allowed the truth to get in the way of a good story, which is why Cleopatra's Needle – that ancient Egyptian monument on London's Embankment – has always retained a name that has nothing to do with reality.

But then everything about Cleopatra's Needle is bizarre. Like most Egyptian artifacts its history is uncertain, but the most likely date for it is around 1500 BC. It was almost certainly commissioned by Thothmes III, whose name appears on the stone. By the year 23 BC it had been moved by Caesar to a position near Cleopatra's Palace, but that is as far as any connection with the great empress goes.

After that it vanishes from history until early in the nineteenth century when it was presented by the local Egyptian ruler as a gift to King George IV. It arrived in London in 1878 after a long campaign to raise enough money to cover the cost of transporting it.

The cost was enormous because the stone is incredibly heavy – 160 tons – and a special case had to be made to move it without damaging it.

Once the obelisk arrived in England there was more trouble – a row immediately started about where it should be put up.

The forecourt of the British Museum was suggested initially; then Kensington Gardens, followed by Greenwich Park, but a site in Parliament Square near the House of

Commons was finally decided on. To convince the doubters – of whom there were many – a wooden replica was first built and erected in the square so that Londoners' reaction could be judged. Then disaster struck – the underground railway company whose line ran under the square was convinced that the obelisk would crash through into their tunnel. This argument was seen as compelling and Parliament Square was rejected. After lengthy further debate the obelisk was moved to its present position by the Thames – appropriate enough, given that it was first built to stand by the edge of the Nile and it now stands, as it has for over a century, on the banks of another great river.

If its journey to England was eccentric the pillar's final placing was even more so. The ancient tradition of burying a child's shoe or a coin beneath a new building for good luck was here taken to ridiculous lengths. Among the objects buried beneath the obelisk – and they are still there – are: a model of the hydraulic equipment used to raise the obelisk; a 2-ft (60-cm) rule; a child's feeding bottle and some toys; a tin of hairpins, some tobacco, a portrait of Queen Victoria, a map of London and a collection of newspapers; a set of coins, several empty jars; copies of the Bible; a translation of the hieroglyphics on the stone; a copy of *Whitaker's Almanack*; a line of rope and some photographs of famous beauties of the day.

The obelisk is a great survivor, however. Having come through the ravages of more than 3,000 years it still bears the marks of bomb damage from the Second World War, and Londoners who grew fond of this oddity in their midst soon came up with a rhyme about it that is somehow both affectionate and dismissive:

This monument as some supposes
Was put up in the time of Moses
It passed in time to the Greeks and Turks
But was put up here by the Board of Works.

PAYING FOR LAND
WITH NAILS

1881

The Law Courts in the Strand were built after a competition to find a suitable design. The architect, G.E. Street (1824–81), won with the Gothic Revival building we see today but the process of implementing the design was dogged by delays caused by some very bizarre architectural requests.

At the outset Street stipulated that standard bricks would be no good for his building, so more than 30 million odd-sized bricks had to be produced at huge cost. The next difficulty was that bricklayers from Germany had to be brought over to complete the work as all London's bricklayers boycotted the work after a row. Street became so concerned about progress on the building that his health declined and he died before the last brick was laid.

But the strangest thing about the law courts is that each year, in a ceremony dating back to the early twelfth century, known as the Rendering of the Quit Rents to the Crown, officials from the Corporation of London come here to pay rent for a piece of ground in Shropshire, owned by the Crown but leased by the Corporation.

The rent is paid in kind: it consists of a billhook and a scythe. Another small patch of ground on Chancery Lane and also owned by the Crown is paid for annually at the law courts in a slightly different way. For this second patch of ground the Corporation of London hands over the princely sum of six horse shoes and 60 nails!

BISMARCK DRUNK ON THE EMBANKMENT

1885

Ever since London's river embankment was completed in the 1880s the authorities have been irritated by the fact that it attracts down-and-outs. With benches set at intervals along its length the Embankment was bound to prove a magnet for the homeless then as now, and among the more illustrious tramps to have slept here are George Orwell (1903–50), who later described life on the road in his unforgettable book *Down and Out in Paris and London*.

That an old Etonian like Orwell should end up destitute on the Embankment is strange enough, but how few people are aware that the greatest German statesman of the nineteenth century, Otto Edward Leopold von Bismarck (1815–98), also slept on a bench on the Embankment?

Bismarck became Chancellor of Germany in 1871 and in 1885 he visited England. As part of the elaborate itinerary organised for his visit, Bismarck was taken – for reasons that have never really become clear – to the long-vanished brewery owned by Barclays in Southwark.

Other dignities and celebrities had been taken to the brewery on many occasions and at the end of such visits the visitor was always asked if he or she would like to try the company's strongest beer. Bismarck was delighted at the idea and was presented with a half-gallon tankard filled to the brim. He should have taken a sip and handed it back but instead, assuming it was all for him, he drank the whole lot.

Perhaps in a spirit of waggishness one of the brewery staff then told the Chancellor that very few men had managed to drink two of the half-gallon flagons. German honour was clearly at stake so Bismarck immediately insisted that the half-gallon flagon be refilled and he proceeded to drink that as well.

Astonishingly he managed to stay on his feet and even to walk in a fairly straight line back to his carriage – the brewery staff apparently applauded him out of the building – which then crossed the river and headed back towards Westminster along the Embankment.

Before they reached Westminster Bridge the Chancellor shouted for the carriage to stop. He looked out of the window, saw the benches by the side of the river and told his assistant that he intended to sleep off the effects of his huge intake of beer. He staggered away to the nearest bench having left instructions that he was to be woken in exactly one hour. His coach, along with the coaches filled with Foreign Office officials, waited patiently at the kerbside while the most famous German statesman in history fell fast asleep on his bench. Exactly one hour later and none the worse apparently for his ordeal he set off for the Foreign Office and some decidedly ticklish discussions about international diplomacy.

ROYAL SCULPTOR WORKS FROM GAOL

1886

There are two bizarre tales about the statue of Queen Anne that stands in front of the entrance to St Paul's Cathedral. It's not the original statue that was completed in 1712 because by the end of the nineteenth century the original was so worn by time, pigeon droppings, coal smog and vandalism that the authorities decided to commission a new statue.

Public sculpture was far more in demand in Victorian England than it is now and many artists whose names mean nothing today were virtually household names a century and more ago.

When a new statue of Queen Anne was needed the City approached the celebrated sculptor Richard Claude Belt. He promised to complete the work in the year it was commissioned – 1886 – but then it all went disastrously wrong. Like many artists Belt was talented but a bit of a reprobate. He was constantly running up debts and getting into scrapes, and about the time he accepted the commission for the new statue of Queen Anne he got into a particularly bad scrape and was imprisoned for fraud. He'd spent the first part of the money advanced for the statue. The city authorities had no intention of throwing that money away by commissioning another artist to start all over again but they couldn't just get Belt released. The answer was to get special permission to deliver stone and tools to Belt's cell!

And that's exactly what happened, with the result that we can confidently say that the St Paul's statue of Queen Anne is the only public work of art completed by a convicted prisoner while he was actually in prison.

Belt's statue was threatened with demolition a few years later when Queen Victoria celebrated her Diamond Jubilee in 1897. The authorities thought that Anne should be removed to make it easier for the royal coach to sweep up to the front of St Paul's so they went ahead with plans to at least move if not simply do away with Belt's statue, but when the Queen heard of the plan she was furious. She is reported to have said: 'If you remove the statue of Queen Anne for me, who is to say that a statue of me will not be removed to accommodate some future monarch after I am dead?' She was no doubt horrified at the thought that the Prince of Wales, the son she loathed and blamed for her husband's death, would become king and then have his revenge on her by getting rid of the dozens of public statues of her that had gone up all over the country during her long reign.

VIOLINIST HIT BY FISH

1890

It's now quite common in London to see geese flying overhead or swans; even, occasionally, a rarity such as a cormorant. Along the Thames right into the heart of the city herons now stalk the shallows and various wildlife bodies tell us that owls roost in Parliament Square while kestrels hover above the Commercial Road.

In the nineteenth century things were very different, as pollution caused by millions of coal fires – not to mention heavy industry – meant there was far less wildlife than today.

But having said that, London's bigger parks have always provided a haven for wildlife, which is why reports of ducks wandering across Kensington High Street with their ducklings coming along behind were always quite common.

Far less common was the bizarre wildlife encounter in Kensington reported in a Victorian newspaper.

Miss Charlotte Wadham, a young and attractive violinist, was walking home one autumn evening after what the delightfully old-fashioned newspaper reporter described as 'a musical engagement involving the celebrated Mr Bach'. She was halfway up Kensington Church Street when she was struck by what she later described to the newspaper as 'a terrific blow to the side of the head'. In fact the bump was so hard that she was knocked unconscious for a few moments.

One of the witnesses who helped the injured woman into a local house where brandy was administered (much, apparently, to the delight of Miss Wadham) described an extraordinary circumstance that almost certainly accounted for the knockout blow. When the witness had run up to the prostrate Miss Wadham he spotted a large fish lying on the pavement nearby. Being a fisherman he knew that this was not the sort of fish one buys at a fishmonger. It was in fact a roach, a common British freshwater fish, but completely inedible. The witness told the newspaper that at first he could not understand how the fish came to be lying in the street, but in helping the injured woman to her feet he noticed something very odd indeed. The woman's head and the shoulder of her coat were dusted here and there with fish scales. The scales were without question from the dead roach found at the scene.

When the newspaper reporter compiled his report on the incident he quoted a professor of zoology who stated that Miss Wadham was almost certainly felled by a roach dropped by a passing bird, possibly a heron or cormorant.

Miss Wadham's violin, much to her relief, was unharmed.

WHY EROS IS ALL WRONG
1893

Londoners often take absolutely no notice of correct terminology. Just because something has an official name doesn't mean it won't end up with a nickname (often an irreverent nickname) – Cleopatra's Needle, for example, has nothing to do with Cleopatra at all but calling it Cleopatra's Needle added an air of romance and the name stuck.

The statue of Eros in Piccadilly is rather similar given that it has absolutely nothing to do with Eros at all. In fact everything about this small, world-famous statue in the centre of Piccadilly is odd. For a start it is made from aluminium, one of the worst metals to withstand the British climate. Then its cupid-style bow is all wrong – bows of this type were strung on the opposite side. As if that were not enough the statue is also facing the wrong way.

The story of this most bizarre statue begins with a fountain built at public expense in memory of one of London's great philanthropists – the seventh Earl of Shaftesbury, after whom Shaftesbury Avenue is named. Shaftesbury spent much of his life and fortune trying to clothe, feed and educate the poor.

The money for the fountain was quickly raised and then some bright spark suggested it should have a statue on top. The money for the statue came pouring in and Alfred Gilbert (1854–1934) was commissioned to design it. Gilbert chose to portray the angel of Christian charity, which is what the statue actually is, but the telltale bow made Londoner's immediately christen it Eros, the god of Love.

The statue was designed to aim its arrow up Shaftesbury Avenue (with which Shaftesbury had been most closely associated) and although it has faced in a number of different directions over the years it has never, ever faced the right way. No one knows why.

The statue was put up and the fountains turned on in 1893 but the basin into which the water fell was too small and the force of water too great – passers-by were soaked and the fountain had to be redesigned almost immediately.

Alfred Gilbert, though now largely forgotten, was hugely influential in the 1880s, but he was as eccentric and bohemian as the statue he designed. He argued about every stage of the work, hated the final result (particularly the fountain on which his sculpture stood) and told the people who'd commissioned him to make the statue that they should take it down, melt it 'and make it into pence to give the unfortunate people who nightly find a resting place on the Thames Embankment to the everlasting shame and disgrace of the greatest metropolis of the world'.

Often short of a penny himself, Gilbert accepted every commission offered to him but hardly ever completed them, simply because he had taken on too much. He eventually had to flee the country or risk being imprisoned for debt.

For the first half-century of its life Eros became an unofficial market place – every day throughout the season flower girls gathered here to sell their wares. They were never removed and were in fact much loved – but after the war, for reasons no one has ever quite been able to fathom, they never returned and the statue is now simply a place where every tourist must have his or her photograph taken.

A RIVER FLYING
THROUGH THE AIR

1895

Sloane Square Station now finds itself in one of London's smartest districts. It lies at one end of what was London's first bus route – buses ran from Sloane Square up Sloane Street to Knightsbridge and back again a distance of less than a mile (1.6km) – but the tube station is nothing out of the ordinary. Built at the end of the nineteenth century as part of the District line, it has always served the wealthy residents of Eaton Square and Belgravia. Like so many pioneering railway builders, the men behind the District line were used to overcoming geological and political difficulties, but they were almost stumped by the difficulties surrounding the building of Sloane Square Station.

When the engineers started work they discovered that a river ran across the path of their proposed railway.

The long-hidden River Westbourne rises to the northwest of Hyde Park (hence Westbourne Terrace) and originally flowed through Hyde Park, enabling eighteenth-century engineers to build the Serpentine. But where the water flows out of the Knightsbridge end of the Serpentine it once continued down towards Sloane Square and on to the Thames.

The railway engineers who built Sloane Square Station were temporarily baffled. Eventually they came up with the solution that still makes Sloane Square one of the strangest stations on the whole underground network.

The engineers built a huge round pipe more than 5ft (1.5m) in diameter to carry the River Westbourne over the platforms and railway lines – anyone who gets off at the station today need only look up to see the massive pipe still in position and the river still runs through it.

Intriguingly it is believed that there may even be a few fish still swimming in the pipe – descendants of the roach, perch and gudgeon that once gathered in the shallows when this was a clean sparkling stream running through open country.

WOOD BARK UNDER THE DISTRICT LINE

1900

When the District line was built beneath the Embankment two of Britain's most powerful lobbying groups – MPs and the legal profession – were not happy. Other landowners had been forced to accept that the new railway would pass under their land because the might of the railway was such that individual objections were always overruled. They had been similarly overruled in earlier decades as the main overground railways opened up even the most remote parts of the country.

But the members of the Inns of Court, from whose ranks MPs, ministers and ultimately members of the House of Lords tend to come, put their collective foot down.

They told the railway engineers that they would not allow trains to run nor tunnels to be dug beneath Parliament Square or beneath the Inns of Court unless extra precautions were taken to ensure that there was no noise and no vibration once the trains began to run.

The railway company knew it was up against some of the most powerful vested interests in the country so they agreed to include a thick layer of finely chopped tree bark immediately beneath the railway track running through the tunnels, but only along those sections that ran through Parliament Square and through the Temple. Even today if you take the District line you will notice that somehow the train runs smoother and more quietly under the MPs and the lawyers.

RITZ CRACKERS

1900

Until well into the twentieth century it was quite common to see people on trains and buses in London carrying shotguns.

Partly this had to do with the fact that when fewer people had cars those who wanted to shoot still had to travel and partly it had to do with the sense that shotguns were not seen as a threat; they were seen as an item of sporting equipment, like a tennis racquet.

In big London hotels, particularly in August, a man with several shotguns under his arm would probably be assumed to be an American on the first leg of a grouse shooting visit, but of course if a gun in a London hotel aroused no interest the same was not true once that gun was fired.

An American visitor to the Ritz at the end of the nineteenth century had all the shooting equipment associated with the very rich – a pair of London guns, the very best shooting clothing and two very expensive looking and well trained dogs. But their owner was from a very rural part of the United States where a man could pretty much walk out the back door of his house and shoot whatever he liked, so when the American visitor noticed small parties of geese and duck flying over the hotel each morning and evening he thought that trying to shoot them was the most natural thing in the world.

Whether he bribed a porter or just managed to find his way to the hotel's rooftop by sheer good luck we don't know, but he was certainly crouching there the following evening and when the first party of duck flew over he managed to get two shots off at them before they veered away and dived for cover.

That first evening he fired two shots and missed both times, but he thought he had the measure of the thing and was convinced he'd have more luck the following evening. As it turned out he was right. With his first shot he downed a mallard that landed on the embankment behind the hotel. It is easy to imagine the excited American running down the stairs and out into the street and then asking the first passer-by if he or she had happened to see a duck fall out of the sky.

The American carried on shooting each evening for five days before an elderly hotel guest complained about the terrible noise each evening from the roof. The management had no idea what the guest was talking about but they sent someone up the following evening and he discovered what was going on. The hotel's reaction to these unusual goings on is not recorded but the shooting stopped and the American was soon on his way to Yorkshire. The hotel management probably had no objection to the shooting itself, only perhaps to the noise and the disturbance of the other guests.

COWS IN THE PARK

1905

Despite the best efforts of developers, London's parks have survived the centuries pretty well. Occasionally roads have sliced through some of them – Park Lane, for example, really was a lane before being turned into a six-lane highway for no good reason. The oldest and most interesting of the parks – St James's – was originally established as a hunting ground so kings and courtiers could hunt deer from the nearby palaces of St James and Westminster.

The point of the hunting grounds was not that they should be big enough to give the deer a sporting chance, but that they should be small enough to guarantee a kill. One of the strangest stories associated with St James's has nothing to do with hunting or indeed with royalty. It concerns the small café that still stands near the lake.

The story begins in 1905 when London's planners decided to build the grand semi-circular Admiralty Arch at the Trafalgar Square end of The Mall. The arch was designed to take up only a small area of what had been open space, but there was a problem. Two elderly women had walked to this corner every day for as long as anyone could remember accompanied by three cows. Having arrived at the edge of the park they tethered their cows and set up stall – for a penny a glass passers-by could enjoy a drink of milk, fresh and still warm from the cow. It was a treat much enjoyed by Londoners and visitors alike and the two women made a very good living. But their place of business was in the way of the new arch and the authorities were not going to let them stand in the way of progress.

They were told to remove themselves forthwith, but word leaked to the press and the public rebelled *en masse* – questions were raised in the House of Commons and the Lords and articles by the great and the good appeared in newspapers saying that it was an outrage to remove one of the most delightful traditions associated with the park. But what clinched it for the two elderly dairymaids was that Edward VII remembered drinking at the ladies' corner and he too thought it was an outrage that they should disappear.

The difficulty was that though the ladies claimed an ancient right to sell milk in the park they had no paperwork to prove it. When questioned by a Commons Committee they insisted their families had sold milk in this corner of the park since the mid-seventeenth century. Researchers got to work and uncovered a long history of milk selling in St James's Park. References in obscure documents dating back centuries did indeed make occasional reference to the sale of milk. It was becoming increasingly difficult to justify the removal of the two milkmaids and their cows.

At last the planners relented and the ladies were allowed to stay but they were told they would have to move away from The Mall and closer to the lake. They were also told that the right to sell milk would die with them. In the end this did not happen, however. The last of the two women died in about 1920 but the sale of refreshments did not die with them. The right to sell refreshments in the park seems to have become a right defined simply by long use and the present kiosk, situated where the two women and their cows once plied their trade, exists under that ancient right.

HIDDEN FIGURES ON
THE BRIDGE

1906

The modernist movement in architecture seems largely to have consisted of a move to ban all forms of decoration from buildings. For the man on the Clapham omnibus, of course, this meant that the built environment that was once designed to delight and entertain both passers-by and those who lived or worked in a particular building suddenly came to look increasingly dull and utilitarian. It is no accident that critics of modernist architecture see it as a close ally of fascism – cold cruel lines, brutal in their conception and execution came to epitomise the most famous architecture of the 1930s onwards and most famously in the work of Le Corbusier and his followers.

The last great flowering of architecture that could be witty and decorative, playful even, came at the end of the much maligned Victorian era. We tend to think of the Victorians as lacking in grace and humour – an entirely false idea. Their builders and architects loved to embellish and decorate even in areas of a building that would only rarely be seen – much as the builders of medieval churches would encourage their carpenters to carve the underside of pews, the Victorians encouraged a riot of decorative stone, wood and brickwork.

One of the most unusual structures in London came about as a result of just this kind of impulse – in 1906 the present Vauxhall Bridge was finally completed. Like all Victorian and earlier bridges across the Thames it is enlivened with decorative detail, but what strange impulse persuaded the designers to add eight sculptures that can only be seen with great difficulty?

On the downstream side of the bridge the figures represent science, local government, education and the fine arts; on the upstream side they represent agriculture, sculpture, pottery and engineering.

Among these extraordinary sculptures is a perfect miniature version of St Paul's held in an outstretched hand!

Little St Paul's on the Water, as it has long been affectionately known among watermen, is very difficult to see from the bridge itself – you have to lean over the parapet, but it is worth it!

BRANDISHING
UMBRELLAS

1910

It is difficult now to understand what all the fuss was about. A small number of intellectuals and professional painters who had enough money to visit France regularly had noticed a revolution taking place in modern painting and they wanted to bring the flavour of that revolution to England where painters of the heavy Victorian academic school still dominated the world of art.

Where great English painters still concentrated on grand scenes from history or detailed academic studies of shipping, interiors, horses, dogs, landscapes or portraits of the good and great, their French and Spanish cousins were using brighter colours to create pictures that did not attempt to tell a story of heroism or tragedy but which existed in and for themselves as interesting, almost abstract designs.

Out went subtle naturalist modelling and grand gestures and in came bright swathes of primary colours; where faces had been meticulously modelled by elderly academicians, the champions of the post impressionist revolution scarcely bothered to fill in the individual features at all.

The figures most closely associated with this revolution in England were the painters Vanessa Bell, Duncan Grant and Roger Fry. Fry organised the first Post-Impressionist exhibition in England in 1910. He hung the work of Cézanne, Simon Bussy, Picasso and others but – being entranced by the vibrant new work – could hardly have expected the furore that ensued.

Art exhibitions, then as now, attracted the well-to-do and the influential and inevitably word got round about an exhibition that was showing new work from the continent. Never thinking what this new work might be like, elderly matrons and delicate spinster aunts turned up at the Grafton Galleries in London on the opening day. Within minutes of the doors opening there were howls of outrage and derision. Umbrellas were – according to Vanessa Bell's son Quentin – brandished, people were struck on the head by elderly matrons convinced they had been morally and physically assaulted, and calls went up for the perpetrators of this outrageous confidence trick to be put in Pentonville Prison. There was, in short, a riot.

Many asked for their money back after insisting that the pictures appeared to have been painted by idiots, pornographers and the insane or at least by people without the least artistic ability or training.

For the newspapers the reaction of an outraged upper middle classes provided fuel for endless stories and the leader writers had a field day condemning the new degenerate art. But of course the first Post-Impressionist exhibition was far more important and significant than that, for despite the outrage, it led to a complete revolution in artistic taste in Britain; a revolution that led ultimately to the popularity and acceptance by the art establishment of *avant garde* artists such as Damien Hirst, Tracey Emin and Jake and Dinos Chapman. Today of course the Post-Impressionists seem tame and very traditional, but they seemed very strange indeed when they first came to London.

ANCIENT HALL
GOES TO CHELSEA
1910

London is constantly changing and in various periods the pace of that change may increase or decrease, but in essence it never stops, which is why buildings built before 1700 are so rare.

Perhaps the most interesting, bizarre and least-known early building is Crosby Hall, which was built near Bishopsgate in the City of London by Sir John Crosby, a wealthy wool merchant. The house was completed between 1466 and 1475 and though it is no longer in Bishopsgate it survives because of the enthusiasm of a group of preservationists in the 1920s.

Crosby Hall now stands in Chelsea near the site of Sir Thomas More's (1478–1535) former home. The hall is largely complete – it has its original roof and oriel window and is the only remaining tangible evidence of how the wealthy built in fifteenth-century London.

It was moved stone by stone in 1910, but is substantially unaltered and the last example left of a medieval London merchant's house. The casual visitor may think as he passes the house on the north bank of the Thames near Cheyne Walk that it is a piece of fake Gothic architecture but he'd be mistaken – this is the real thing.

ONE-LEGGED ESCALATOR TESTER

1911

London's underground railway system is the oldest in the world and many of the tunnels we travel through today are relatively unchanged from when they were first built late in the nineteenth or early in the twentieth century.

When the Piccadilly line opened in 1906 it was the longest underground line in the world, covering more than 10 miles (16.1km). It was later extended to 32 miles (51.5km) and then finally covered more than 40 miles (64.4km), but even at 10 miles it was one of the wonders of the world – it was also rather terrifying for passengers unused to travelling below ground.

But hardly had the public got used to this remarkable long-distance underground railway than the company that ran the trains introduced something even more remarkable.

When London's first railway escalator began operating at Earl's Court Station on the Piccadilly line in 1910 the passengers, to a man, were too terrified to use it. The railway company was aghast – they'd paid huge sums to have the revolutionary equipment fitted but it was all wasted if no one would dare use it. Then a bright spark had an idea – why not employ someone to use the escalator throughout the day to give the public confidence? The idea was accepted and Bumper Harris, a man with a wooden leg, was thereafter employed for a number of years to go up and down the escalator all day. Soon the public began to realise that if a man with one leg could use this remarkable new transportation system safely there was no reason why they shouldn't be able to. Of course Bumper, about whom almost nothing else is known, did his job too well – the public soon thought nothing of using the new moving staircase and he was out of a job.

THE STATUE
THAT ISN'T THERE
1912

When Peter Llewellyn Davies, a successful publisher, killed himself in 1960 by throwing himself under a train at Sloane Square, the newspaper headlines were all variations on a theme and that theme was Peter Pan.

Llewellyn Davies, like his four brothers, had been the inspiration for what is one of the most famous characters in children's fiction.

Peter Pan came into existence almost by accident when author J.M. Barrie (1860–1937) met the Llewellyn Davies boys in Kensington Gardens in 1900. He befriended their mother and father and when both died of cancer, Barrie virtually took over the boys' upbringing. He showered them with gifts and paid for their education. The games they played together in Kensington Gardens inspired the story of the boy who never grew up.

Years later the only surviving brother, Nico, told an interviewer that Barrie's motives were not sexual. But there is no doubt that Barrie was an unhappy man who wished to live vicariously, as it were, through the boys he idolised. Certainly his own marriage was a disaster and there were rumours that it was never consummated, for Barrie seems to have loved the idea of being in love – particularly with young actresses – rather than the reality of it.

When *Peter Pan* was first performed in London in 1904 it made Barrie famous – and very rich. In 1912 he conceived the idea of a statue of Peter Pan in the park where he had first played with the Llewellyn Davies boys, but this proved difficult and complex. Statues in the royal parks are permitted only following agreement by Royal Commission or, at the least, a parliamentary committee. But Barrie was world famous by now and not an easy man to refuse. After making enquiries he received an extremely odd reply to his request to erect the statue. He was told that he would not receive permission, but at the same time there would be no objection. On that basis Barrie assumed he could go ahead so he commissioned Sir George Frampton (1860–1928) to make the statue we see today.

J.M. Barrie himself unveiled the new statue at midnight and on his own – he liked the idea that children would see it the next morning and assume it had simply appeared as if by magic.

Initially the statue was hated (though not by children) but by 1921 it was the most popular statue in London, a position it almost certainly retains to this day.

But the lives of the boys who inspired the story and the statue were curiously unhappy – despite material wealth and expensive private educations provided by the ever generous Barrie, they seem to have been deeply troubled. Michael Llewellyn Davies, Barrie's favourite of the five brothers, drowned with a close friend during his last year at Oxford. There were rumours that it was a suicide pact and it is certainly true that Michael drowned at a spot on the river where only a good swimmer should have been – Michael could not swim at all. George was killed in action during the First World War and Peter, as we have seen, committed suicide. In Peter's case the connection with Barrie and the story of Peter Pan was almost certainly central to his decision to end his life.

In 1952 he had burned more than 2,000 letters between his brother Michael and Barrie – he called the collection of letters 'The Morgue' and told friends that he absolutely

J.M. Barrie himself unveiled the new statue at midnight and on his own – he liked the idea that children would see it the next morning and assume it had simply appeared as if by magic.

loathed the connection with Barrie. It is odd that something that has brought so much pleasure to countless thousands of children across the world should have brought only sorrow to the five children who inspired it. Curious too that their memorial, the statue of Peter Pan, is a statue that, officially at least, isn't even there.

THE PALACE THAT FACES
THE WRONG WAY
1912

Buckingham Palace is known throughout the world as the
London home of the royal family, but it has a curious and
less well-known history. The present building is the fourth
on the site and it started life as a small, rather unpretentious
house lived in by the Duke of Buckingham.

Built at the end of the seventeenth century, the original
house bore no resemblance to the present building.
Buckingham sold it in 1761 to George III, who wanted it for
his wife Charlotte. Some 14 of George's 15 children were
born in the house.

William Chambers (1723–96) was brought in to partly
rebuild and remodel the house in 1762 and it was left alone
then until the 1820s when John Nash (1752–1835) doubled
the size of the main block and refaced the house with Bath
stone. He demolished a couple of wings and had Marble
Arch made as a triumphal entrance to a new courtyard –
Marble Arch was then discovered to be too narrow for the
royal coach. One would have thought that the designers
would have measured a coach or two before going ahead
– they didn't because they wanted the arch to be an exact
copy of the Roman Triumphal Arch of Constantine. George
IV and his architect John Nash wanted to reflect the dignity
of ancient Rome, but in their obsession with ancient
precedent they forgot modern practicality. The width of the
arch itself is perfect for a Roman chariot but far too narrow

for a Georgian coach. The embarrassing arch was moved in 1851 to an isolated spot at the end of the Edgware Road and there it has stayed ever since. And still to this day only royal coaches are allowed to go through the arch – except, of course, they don't fit so it remains unused.

But back to Buckingham House. After spending more than £500,000 of taxpayers' money (the budget was £150,000) on it George IV died in 1830 having never actually lived in the house. His 'improvements' were still unfinished. The new king, William IV, spent more money on the house.

It's easy to forget that before Queen Victoria and the growth in which they took part of newspapers, which brought a sense of the monarch as a public figure, the royal family did not care what the general public thought of them. They lived private lives and the grand public ceremonies were only ever seen by other important people. If a king spent too much money on a project no one would dare criticise them anyway, although Parliament might grumble.

But as the monarchy realised that its public role was developing and that it had to show its face to the world, a decision was taken to turn Buckingham Palace around so that instead of facing into its private park it would face down The Mall in a decidedly public manner. This is why what we think of as the front of the palace is actually the back – the 'real' front faces the private park as it has always done.

It was Victoria who had the east front added in the 1840s by Edward Blore (1787–1879). For the first time the house faced down The Mall. But the endless tampering with the house didn't end there – Blore's French stone was considered too soft so it was replaced a few decades later by the architect Sir Aston Webb (1849–1930) using the rather harsh Portland stone we see today.

A CARRIAGE PULLED
BY ZEBRAS

1920

Aristocrats traditionally have the time and the money to indulge the most obscure, eccentric tastes. And the combination of money and eccentricity has always produced Londoners of exceptional lunacy.

Take Walter Rothschild (1868–1937), for example. Decidedly but brilliantly eccentric, he hated speaking to people, was blackmailed out of a fortune by his mistress and trained three zebras to pull his carriage along Pall Mall. Unfitted for the normal routes into public life that Rothschild elder sons tended to take, he set up a natural history museum that eventually grew into the biggest private museum in the world.

Throughout his life he was prepared to pay almost anything for a rare or unusual specimen, and by 1920, after working in virtual seclusion for years for 18 hours a day, he had amassed some 2,000 complete mounted animals, 200 animal heads, 300 sets of antlers, 3,000 stuffed birds, 700 reptiles, 1,000 stuffed fish, 300,000 bird skins and 200,000 birds' eggs. He was a brilliant if utterly obsessive zoological classifier – his enthusiasm and dedication was eventually rewarded when a subspecies of giraffe was named after him.

The stories of his madcap adventures in London are legion. Among the best is the story of his motorcar outing in Hyde Park. He was hurtling through the park and had reached the bridge over the Serpentine when he spotted a chauffeur standing outside a stationary car with a folded rug over his arm. Rothschild immediately shouted at his own driver to stop. He leaped from the car, explaining that the rug in the other chauffeur's arms was made from the pelts of extremely rare tree kangaroos. Having waited until the owner of the rug arrived he refused to leave until the rug had been sold to him – the owner of the rug was shrewd enough to demand an absurdly high price but Rothschild would have paid almost anything.

PRIME MINISTER CAUGHT IN A BROTHEL?

1926

No one really knows why clubs started in London, but the whole idea of like-minded people getting together regularly to discuss mutual interests seems to have been, in its origins, peculiarly British and the very first clubs were certainly based in London.

The first clubs included the Wolf Club, whose only qualification for membership was that a man had to have been forbidden to sing in the bath by his wife (see page 121); the Lunar Society (whose scientifically minded members met when there was a full moon); the Fly Fishers' Club, whose members were addicted to pursuing trout by the most difficult means possible; the Garrick, where actors and those in the media were able to boast to each other about how wonderful they were; the Macaroni Club, whose members, according to one critic, were 'upper-class effeminate practitioners of sodomy, a crime imported from Italy by our spindle-shanked Gentry, who make the grand Tour but to bring home the vices of our Neighbours, and return, if possible, greater Coxcombs than they were before Embarkation'; and the Beefsteak, originally known as the Sublime Society of Steaks. It began in 1735 and is still based in Irving Street. Its founder members met to discuss the disgraceful tendencies of 'levelling' – by which they meant the tendency, which cannot have been that common in early eighteenth-century London, for different classes to mix.

Beefsteak members were the supreme reactionaries who believed that birth conferred a status that neither success nor failure in life could change.

By 1926 the club was still meeting and some of Britain's most powerful reactionaries were members. Unfortunately, they met in an old, rather seedy, house on the edge of Soho and at a time when the police were taking a more than usually enthusiastic interest in local brothels.

On one particular summer evening a policeman saw four elderly and rather disreputable-looking men enter a house. The policeman made a written note to the effect that 'They looked highly suspicious and eager not to be observed'. The policeman called for reinforcements, convinced that they were about to raid a brothel. They forced their way into the house and arrested the four men, who happened to be the Governor of the Bank of England, the Chancellor of the Exchequer, the Prime Minister and the Archbishop of Canterbury.

When their identities were revealed the arresting policemen refused to believe them and threatened them with further prosecution for attempting to impersonate their betters! Despite the best efforts of the Beefsteak Club it seems that class isn't always that obvious!

THE WORLD'S MOST FAMOUS PARROT

1926

Archaeology is not just about discovering how the great lived or worshipped. It's also about how the poor lived – but as the poor tend to have less they have tended to leave fewer artifacts in the archaeological record. Which is why an occasional commonplace survival from an earlier era deserves the attention it often gets. One such survival is the Cheshire Cheese public house just off London's Fleet Street.

In 1666 the Great Fire of London destroyed Old St Paul's, crept down Ludgate Hill towards the River Fleet and even destroyed a number of houses on the west of the river in what is today Fleet Street. But a few houses did escape the flames only to be destroyed – for example – when the hideous modern buildings of King's College were built.

Fleet Street was always famously bordered by a mass of tangled courts and alleyways typical of a crowded city that had grown slowly over many centuries.

Most of these courts and alleys are now built over or lined with dull office buildings but in Wine Office Court there is a most surprising survivor – a late seventeenth-century pub that looks exactly inside as it would have looked when it was first built. What's more, the interior is not a re-creation – the tables in the public bar, the fireplace, the décor and the pictures on the wall have all been here for at least 200 years.

The fame of the Cheshire Cheese spread far and wide and from the
1850s it was on the itinerary of most visitors to London.

If we compare the interior of the Cheshire Cheese to prints and drawings of early London coffee houses we realise that the Cheese is the last of these long-vanished and once hugely popular features of London life.

The fame of the Cheshire Cheese spread far and wide and from the 1850s it was on the itinerary of most visitors to London. And by 1900 the pub had a resident who was to become almost as famous as the Cheese itself – this was Polly the Eccentric Parrot. Polly was known across the world for her bizarre antics and for her intelligence and abilities as a mimic. Famously garrulous and rude about visitors she didn't like, Polly celebrated the end of the First World War in 1918 in her own way. She imitated the noise of champagne corks popping an estimated 400 times and then fell off her perch suffering from exhaustion.

When she died in 1926 she was estimated to be over 40 and her antics over the years she spent at the Cheshire Cheese earned her an accolade unique in the animal kingdom – her obituary appeared in more than 200 newspapers worldwide.

Polly lived at the Cheese during its most famous days but the list of celebrities who drank here is extraordinary: mostly literary figures are associated with the pub – Dr Johnson, who lived just two minutes' walk away in Gough Square, is reported to have come here every night for years along with his friend and biographer James Boswell (1740–95); Dickens sat through many long evenings in the corner by the door in the room opposite the public bar; in the eighteenth century the actor and impresario David Garrick (1717–79) came here with his friends the painter Sir Joshua Reynolds (1723–92) and Edward Gibbon (1737–94), author of *The Decline and Fall of the Roman Empire*; in the nineteenth century as well as Dickens, Wilkie Collins (1824–89) was a regular together with Tennyson (1809–92) and Carlyle (1795–1881); by the twentieth century everyone from Theodore Roosevelt (1858–1919) to Mark Twain (1835–1910) and Conan Doyle (1859–1930) came.

Above the fireplace in the public bar is a fascinating portrait dating from 1829, darkened by the smoke from countless candles and coal fires, of the waiter William Simpson. Apart from the fact that paintings of servants are rare the picture is interesting because the very table on which Simpson leans in his portrait is still in the bar nearby.

In the nineteenth century, the Cheese had one other claim to eccentricity: its landlord made some of the biggest pies in London. Filled with beef, oysters and lark each pie weighed between 50 and 80lb (23–36.kg)! Each was big enough to feed about 100 people and among those who ceremonially dished up the first serving were Sir Arthur Conan Doyle and future Prime Minister Stanley Baldwin (1867–1947).

ENTERTAINER WITH A POTATO HEAD

1929

In his famous book *Down and Out in Paris and London* (published in 1933) George Orwell recounts the extraordinary number of ways in which London's destitute managed to earn a living, from the screevers who drew pictures on the paving stones outside galleries and public buildings to the singers, acrobats, jugglers and escapologists. Orwell – himself an old Etonian – met several other old Etonians who were destitute and sleeping rough on London's streets.

But among the odd characters he meets none is perhaps more extraordinary than the big bald-headed Irishman who made a very decent living outside London's theatres using nothing more than a large potato.

We have to remember that before the telephone was widely available many theatregoers, if not most, would queue outside the theatre to buy tickets for that evening's performance. This meant that street entertainers had something of a captive audience.

The Irishman with the potato had a very simple and effective routine. He attracted the attention of the crowd, threw his potato (the biggest he could find) high into the air and then manoeuvred himself until he was directly underneath it. When the potato hit his bald head it splattered into tiny pieces and the Irishman immediately went along the queue with his hat.

Hard though it may be to believe, the audiences loved it.

A STATUE
WITH ITS OWN INCOME

1929

St Dunstan's Church in Fleet Street is one of London's oddest churches. For a start it is octagonal in shape – the result of an oddly shaped site – and for many years it provided a home to a number of strange Christian sects: the Coptic Ethiopian Church, the Assyrian Church, the Romanian Orthodox Church and the Old Catholic Church of Utrecht. Now hemmed in on all sides by later rebuilding, the churchyard was once a thriving place of business. Anyone who has a collection of seventeenth-and eighteenth-century books will see on the title page again and again the address 'Published at St Dunstan's in the West' followed by the date, for St Dunstan's, like St Paul's less than a mile (1.6km) away, was once a great centre of book publishing.

The most reprinted book after the Bible was first printed here – Izaak Walton's *The Compleat Angler* (far more a book about the contemplative life than about fishing) was sold here by Walton himself, who lived here and was St Dunstan's churchwarden for many years.

But the strangest feature of St Dunstan's is the statue of Elizabeth I that stands just in front of the church. Carved in the 1580s while the Queen was still alive it stood for many years on Ludgate where the Queen would regularly have seen it on her progresses from Westminster to the City and back. When Ludgate was demolished at the end of the eighteenth century the statue was brought to St Dunstan's.

The statue has been here ever since and it is the only statue in London (probably the only statue in the world) that has its own income.

In 1929 the philanthropist Lady Millicent Fawcett, concerned that the statue should be properly looked after, left £700 in trust for it to be cleaned and repaired in perpetuity.

FISHING FROM THE ROOF
OF THE SAVOY

1930

The Savoy Hotel and surrounding area is rich in history, much of it bizarre in the extreme, but there are also odd endearing tales that attach themselves to the modern hotel and the ancient palace that once stood on the Thameside site.

One of the best of these tales concerns two guests staying at the hotel back in the 1930s.

Like the English, Americans are obsessed with fishing with rod and line and to the enthusiast half the pleasure of fishing is arguing about flies and lines and the various techniques for casting them.

Two Americans staying at the Savoy in London were particularly keen on fishing and over dinner one evening they had an argument over whether or not it would be possible to cast a fly, using a salmon rod, from the roof of their hotel over the gardens and the busy Embankment and into the Thames.

They were so determined to settle the dispute that they went along to Hardy Brothers, the tackle-makers in Pall Mall, and asked them to decide if such a thing was possible. Hardy Brothers approached the angler and author Esmond Drury who agreed to attempt the feat on condition that he was tied securely to a chimney on the hotel roof.

Early one Sunday morning, and with the help of a policeman who stopped all the traffic on the Embankment, he proved that it was indeed possible to cast a fly into the Thames from the roof of the Savoy.

But the Savoy has always been a place that generates eccentricities. Take the short street at the front where taxis pull up to pick up hotel guests – this short stretch of roadway is the only place in the country where traffic is allowed to drive on the wrong side of the road. No one knows why this is but cars and taxis here must drive on the right.

The Savoy stands on the site of the old medieval Savoy Palace built by Henry III's friend Count Peter of Savoy in 1264. The courtyard at the front of the present hotel is said to follow the lines of the original medieval courtyard palace. The present building, completed in 1889, was commissioned and paid for by Richard D'Oyly Carte (1844–1901) using the vast sums he made putting on Gilbert and Sullivan operas. The famous Peach Melba was invented here (in honour of the great opera diva Nellie Melba), as was the dry martini. And legend has it that if 13 guests find themselves about to sit down to supper the hotel will provide a fourteenth guest (a black cat) to avoid the bad luck inherent in the number 13.

And there is a long tradition at the hotel that if the guest is important enough they will put up with almost anything – one guest turned up with her pet crocodile, others have appeared with monkeys; marmosets and parrots are virtually commonplace. Two final strange tales about the Savoy: an American guest once took pot shots with his 12-bore shotgun from the roof at geese flying towards Green Park, and the great violinist Jascha Heifetz once had bagpipe lessons on the roof.

A little further west along the Strand from the Savoy is a short street that once ran down to the river. Savoy Street will take you to the Savoy Chapel, parts of which certainly date back to the original foundation, which is contemporaneous with Count Peter's twelfth-century palace. Most of the present building is relatively recent but it was once the cause of a bizarre legal suit. Having reverted to the Crown following the death of Peter of Savoy (1203–68) the chapel was given to the Duke of Lancaster – who also happened to be the king. This meant the chapel was owned both by the king and by the Duke of Lancaster, but as they were one and the same person confusion reigned. The difficulty was only eliminated in the early eighteenth century when the king sued the Duke (i.e. he sued himself) to establish who had the right to the chapel and the land on which it was built. Not surprisingly the king won.

THE BUILDING
THAT'S REALLY AN
ADVERTISEMENT

1930

In the early part of the twentieth century, London was still a rather strait-laced place where advertising was considered rather vulgar – to the extent that it was banned on the sides of buildings.

Partly this was an attempt to tidy up after the chaos of earlier centuries when shopkeepers and tradesmen put signs outside their shops and then tried to outdo each other by gradually making their signs bigger or attaching them to long poles until narrow streets would be dark all day because of the shadows cast by countless signs.

The first buses were also covered in ads, which then began to creep up the sides of buildings until the authorities called a halt. Tall buildings began to appear and though they would have provided magnificent sites for advertisements the authorities were horrified at the prospect. But one or two advertisers were determined to get round the ban and in at least one strange instance they got away with it.

On the south bank near Blackfriars Bridge a tower was built above a warehouse. The tower still survives and is now home to a very fashionable restaurant which offers diners a magnificent view from their tables along the river. At the top of the tower and visible from miles away there is an advertisement for the famous Oxo beef cube. The ad has been here since the building was first put up and it escaped the ban to which all such similar ads would have been subject. It did it by incorporating the advertisement – the letters OXO – into the very structure of the building. What look like three big letters are in fact three gigantic windows filled with red glass.

COWS IN THE STRAND

1930

Until relatively recently all London's food supplies had to be brought fresh to the capital – in the days before refrigeration there was no alternative, which explains why live animals were driven to Smithfield well into the twentieth century and milk was sold in various parks around London straight from the cow. Until 1900 you might often have seen a flock of geese marching towards London, each bird wearing a pair of tar boots (their feet were dipped in tar to prevent the long walk causing bleeding and pain).

But London was also a curiously unregulated place and the authorities were often more astonished than anyone to discover that odd trades and crafts were still being carried on long after everyone had assumed they were extinct.

Down by the river about halfway between Waterloo and Charing Cross Bridges was the world's first block of flats. Adelphi Terrace, completed in 1768, was built by the Adam brothers and was split into apartments – to the utter astonishment of Londoners who had never seen anything like it before.

Sadly little remains of this marvellous scheme and the superb buildings that once stood here. Most were demolished in the 1930s (one part survives in nearby Adam Street) but it was discovered as demolition got under way that an elderly woman was still living in the building along with half a dozen cows whose milk she sold in the Strand!

Dozens of other curious tales attach to this most historic and relatively little-altered part of London – J.M. Barrie of *Peter Pan* fame and George Bernard Shaw, for example, lived opposite each other for a while in Robert Street and when they wanted a break from writing they would throw biscuits or cherry stones at each other's windows to attract attention.

Another story tells how the Adam brothers wanted the building work on the Adelphi carried out as cheaply as possible so they brought workers down from Scotland. The workers quickly found out how much less than the going rate they were being paid and went on strike, so the brothers set off for Ireland where they employed Irish labourers, but only those who could speak no English! But the canny Irish, though they spoke only Gaelic, were not so easily fooled. Within days of their starting work in London they knew they were being swindled – the Adam brothers forgot that many of the workers would have had relatives in London and they quickly discovered what they should have been paid. In the face of another threat of strike action the Adam brothers quietly gave in and paid up.

MAX MILLER'S LAST
PERFORMANCE

1936

Much of what once made London a truly fascinating place has been destroyed in the name of profit. The Victorians were particularly bad at knocking anything and everything down for this reason but we have not learned by their bad example. When the grossly overpaid and incompetent officials at the Royal Opera House wanted to make their theatre bigger and therefore more profitable in the 1980s they destroyed a row of eighteenth-century buildings, including the house in which Tom's Coffee Shop – one of the best-known coffee houses in eighteenth-century London – opened in 1722.

The much-loved buildings of the old Covent Garden Market were only just saved following a campaign by local residents in the late 1970s. Developers didn't care a fig for the historic fabric of the area. In the 1930s a similar campaign to save the world-famous old Alhambra Theatre in Leicester Square was not so successful, but the destruction of this splendid old building (since replaced by the Odeon Leicester Square) led to one of the oddest and saddest of all goodbyes.

The great comedian Max Miller (1894–1963), who was banned by the BBC for telling rude jokes, heard that the Alhambra, one of his favourite theatres, was being demolished so he went along to have a last look at the building in which he'd performed on numerous occasions.

He arrived at lunchtime and hearing that the famous stage was to be taken down that afternoon he climbed on to the boards and gave the workmen an impromptu – and by all accounts hilarious – one-hour performance. Ten minutes after he'd finished, the stage was gone for ever.

Towards the end of his life Miller confessed that in a distinguished career his proudest moment was not appearing on the BBC or at the Theatre Royal but, as he put it, 'closing the old Alhambra'

TOP-SECRET GRASS-CUTTING SERVICE

1940

In its present triumphal form The Mall was laid out in the nineteenth century to emulate the triumphal routes of various other capitals – for example, Paris and Rome. It joins Trafalgar Square to Buckingham Palace, passing Horse Guards Parade on the way. The Mall is a familiar thoroughfare, but just where it passes Horse Guards Parade there is a very odd building that most people completely fail to notice.

Built from dark-red bricks and almost always covered in ivy, the Admiralty Citadel as it is called, has a fortress feel about it – there is no decorative brickwork and not a ground-floor window in sight.

The building was made to protect the admiralty communications centre from bombs during the Second World War and almost nothing about it appears in any guide book about London.

When it was first put up the press was forbidden to mention it and everything possible was done to make sure it was undetectable, particularly from the air, and impregnable. The walls are incredibly thick and there is no doubt that it would withstand a conventional bomb or two, but just to be on the safe side the military decided that the best way to hide the building from the air would be to plant grass on top of it.

However, this led to one extremely eccentric proceeding which continues to this day – every morning in summer an employee carrying his top-secret pass presents himself to the officials within the building and is allowed to enter. He carries with him a lawn mower – this has to be carried out through an upstairs window onto a set of steps that lead to the roof. He mows the grass, carries his mower back downstairs across the office floor and out of the building.

HOW ST PAUL'S HAD
A MIRACULOUS ESCAPE
1940

The Blitz on London – the word is from the German *Blitzkrieg* meaning 'lightning war' – destroyed almost as much of the beautiful ancient City as the planners and developers of the 1950s and 1960s.

Despite its great size and the fact that, from the air, St Paul's Cathedral was an easy target, London's greatest church was not destroyed during the Blitz – in fact it was scarcely touched at all, despite the rain of bombs that fell in the area month after month. The fact of St Paul's survival is well known, but it is only when we look in detail at the number and size of bombs that fell that we realise quite what a miraculous escape the church had.

The bombing began in September 1940. Before that date Hitler had concentrated his attacks on British RAF fields and more obviously military targets, but the indiscriminate bombing of London that began in September showed that Hitler would stop at nothing to win the war. His actions over London and later Coventry were to lead ultimately to the fire bombing of Dresden and other horrors.

For 57 nights London was bombed every night and frequently also during the day. Between September 1940 and May 1941 almost 19,000 tons of high explosive rained down on the capital. Largely residential areas such as Southwark and Holborn were very badly damaged.

Through the early weeks of the Blitz the historic area of smaller houses and offices that were in many cases just yards from St Paul's in a warren of tiny ancient streets were completely flattened by direct hits. The whole of the historic booksellers' area of Paternoster Row vanished forever, but right in the midst of this firestorm St Paul's remained unscathed for reasons that really cannot be adequately explained – expert fire watching certainly helped and the cathedral was also just very lucky. Disaster came very close indeed when on 12 September a bomb fell right next to the southwest tower but failed to explode. It buried itself deep underground and hard up against the church foundations – only the skill and bravery of the firefighters who spent three days extricating the bomb prevented disaster. When the bomb was finally removed it was still live. It was placed on the back of a truck and carried at a snail's pace to Hackney Marshes where it was detonated – the resulting crater measured more than 100ft (30.5m) across.

WHY THE AMERICANS DON'T OWN THEIR EMBASSY

1950

Despite London's apparent pride in its built heritage, early buildings are still demolished to make way for the bland and the mediocre. Most recently the Mappin and Webb site – a group of attractive Victorian City buildings from the nineteenth century – was destroyed to make way for yet more bland office buildings; in the 1970s and 1980s Georgian and earlier houses in central London were frequently pulled down for no good reason. But even while the authorities were allowing the destruction to go ahead they were extolling the virtues to tourists of London's historic architecture – the very architecture they were allowing to be demolished at every opportunity.

But it was far worse in the past. In the 1920s all of John Nash's magnificent Regent Street was demolished; in the 1870s the last great Jacobean mansion in central London – Northumberland House – was destroyed to build, of all things, a cut-through road.

In the 1930s Norfolk House, an exquisite building in St James's Square, was knocked down to build something of no merit whatsoever. The list goes on almost indefinitely.

Grosvenor Square, between Piccadilly and Oxford Street, suffered particularly badly from this mania for destruction. By the 1940s most of the original houses in the square – many relatively unaltered since the late seventeenth century – had gone to be replaced by flats and shops.

Then, in the late 1950s, the Duke of Westminster agreed to allow the Americans to demolish the whole of the west side of the square so they could put up the terrible building we see today; but the siting of the American Embassy led to one of the most bizarre and protracted processes of negotiation ever seen in London.

The Americans have embassies all over the world and in every single case they buy the land first and then build their embassy. They assumed that this would be possible in England so they asked the Duke of Westminster – who owned Grosvenor Square – how much they would have to pay to buy the freehold of the land. What they didn't know is that the Grosvenor family never sell. Their vast wealth is based precisely on this simple fact: they own 300 acres (121ha) of central London including most of Belgravia and Mayfair, not to mention land holdings all over the world. All the houses and offices on this land are leased; their freeholds are never sold.

When the Americans were told they could not buy their land they insisted that was unacceptable and that they would petition Parliament to force the Duke to sell. Questions were asked in Parliament; the Grosvenor family were heavily leaned on but all to no avail.

Then the Duke thought of a good compromise. He told the furious Americans that if they were prepared to return to the Grosvenor family all those lands in the United States stolen after the American War of Independence then he would allow the Americans to buy their site on the west side of Grosvenor Square. The Americans knew when they were beaten (they would have had to give the Duke most of Maine and New York!) and being unwilling to hand over land they themselves had stolen from the Indians anyway, they backed down and the Duke of Westminster allowed them a 999-year lease. And that explains why the embassy in London is the only American embassy built on land not owned by the United States.

A GIFT TO LONDON – A GERMAN LAMPPOST

1963

The practice of town twinning is bizarre – for many it simply provides an excuse for local officials to enjoy all-expenses-paid trips overseas; for those who enjoy such trips, twinning represents (perhaps) a hand of friendship extended across the seas to nations with whom we are already friendly.

Perhaps the slightly dubious nature of twinning explains one of the strangest gifts ever given by one nation to another.

Anyone who walks along the north side of the Thames above Hammersmith Bridge will see the old inns and boathouses that have characterised the area for centuries, but tucked away against the wall of an old house the eagle-eyed may spot something very different – a worn rectangular metal plaque. The plaque records that in 1963 Herr Willy Brandt (1913–92), later the German Chancellor, gave the good citizens of Hammersmith a lamppost. The gift was to mark the twinning of Hammersmith with the borough of Neukölln in Berlin. The plaque declares that 'The lamp above this plaque was formerly used to light a street in West Berlin. It was presented by Herr Willy Brandt, the Mayor of West Berlin, to councillor Stanley Atkins as a token of friendship.'

Whether the lamp has some symbolic significance – perhaps to shed light on the relationship or to illuminate the dark past of European history is anyone's guess. One wonders what Hammersmith gave West Berlin – perhaps a manhole cover or a stretch of municipal railing!

CAMPAIGNING AGAINST PEANUTS AND SITTING

1965

Strange stories and strange characters are not entirely a feature of London's more distant past. Anyone over 50 who knows London well will remember a very odd character who haunted Oxford Street and Regent Street for several decades.

Stanley Green died at the age of 78 in 1992, having spent nearly 30 years parading the West End carrying a placard warning mostly against the dangers of protein.

Over the years he sold tens of thousands of hand-printed leaflets (at 12p each) explaining why lustful feelings were induced by 'fish, birds, meat, cheese, egg, peas, beans, nuts and sitting'. He had worked for many years in a perfectly ordinary job in the civil service before starting his one-man campaign against lust and peanut eating in the early 1960s.

No one really knows why he decided that protein was the root of all the world's evils but once he'd made his decision he never gave up.

'Protein makes passion,' he would say to anyone who would listen. 'If we eat less of it, the world will be a happier place.'

He produced his leaflets on a small press in his tiny flat in northwest London; the tenants below often complained about the terrific sounds of thumping and crashing on print day. Until he qualified for a free bus pass he would cycle each day to Oxford Street in his raincoat, cap and wire-rimmed spectacles, and always recalled with pleasure that motorists reading the board on the back of his bicycle would toot their horns and wave. 'I've known coaches pass,' he said, 'and everyone has stood up and cheered me.'

He was occasionally spat at, but he was rarely upset by abuse, explaining that people only attacked him because they thought he was a religious person, which he most clearly was not. He would often concentrate his efforts on cinema queues, using such opening gambits as 'You cannot deceive your groom that you are a virgin on your wedding night.'

CABMAN'S REVENGE

1965

For centuries London's cabmen and porters were vital to the efficient running of the city, but as long as they continued their work nothing much was thought of them. In the eighteenth century this began to change when a porter's rest was put up in Piccadilly – this strange-looking contraption is a broad, thick plank of wood set on two cast-iron pillars. The plank would be at chest or even shoulder height for the average man. The reason it was fixed at this height is that it allowed the porters to ease any load off their shoulders and on to the plank, which was almost at the same height, rather than have to lower it to any significant extent. The porter's rest allowed them to slip their load off and on again easily.

Hansom cabs were the great feature of the second half of the nineteenth century (particularly after Poet Laureate Sir John Betjeman's grandfather invented a new lock for their doors) and they grew massively in numbers until the advent of the First World War – after 1918 they rapidly disappeared as motor cabs took over.

But the harsh conditions under which the Victorian hansom-cab drivers had to work – out in all weathers for 12 or more hours a day, seven days a week – came to the attention of a group of philanthropists who started the cabmen's shelter fund in 1874. Their money was used to establish a set of green timber buildings – usually set in the middle of broad thoroughfares – where the cabmen could stop for a cup of tea or lunch or dinner. Many of these cabmen's shelters have now disappeared but thankfully those that remain are now protected. They are always painted green and look rather like large slightly ornate garden sheds with small windows and a pitched roof.

One such cabmen's shelter survives in the Brompton Road near Knightsbridge. Another can be found just off Sloane Street. A third, in Temple Place just north of the Embankment, was the cause of one of the oddest building disputes of the past two centuries.

When in the 1960s a proposal was lodged by developers to knock down four ancient streets running down to Temple Place, officials at the Greater London Council agreed to allow the demolition despite the fact that the hotel planned for the site was designed to house tourists who presumably were coming to London to see the sort of sites their hotel was about to destroy.

The disgraceful demolition plan got the go-ahead and the vast hotel was built but as it neared completion the dozy architects realised that just at the spot they'd planned to put their grand hotel entrance there was a green cabmen's shelter.

With typical corporate stupidity they tried to use their financial might to have the shelter removed by the authorities, but they were told that the shelter had been there since 1880 and it was staying put. Filled with horror that their rich American clients would baulk at the sight of a ramshackle old cab shelter in front of their new hotel, the directors of the building firm had to approach the cabmen cap in hand and ask if they would mind if their shelter were moved a few yards down the street. The cabmen – far more civilised than the corporate bigwigs – agreed provided that the hotel owners paid for the shelter to be moved and made a donation to the cabmen's shelter fund. No doubt the hotel paid as little into the fund as they could, but the shelter was duly – and very carefully – moved a few yards along the road.

'HOW NOT TO GET LOST IN LIBERTY'S'

1970

One of London's most famous shops since it was opened by Arthur Liberty, a Buckinghamshire draper, in 1875, Liberty's was the ultimate in fashion between 1880 and 1920 and it has always been associated with the Arts and Crafts movement. The shop originally sold Japanese fans – Mr Liberty was one of the first to import oriental goods as well as silks and other fabrics in bulk.

Then in 1925, flushed with success, the company, which had by now acquired three adjacent shops, decided to rebuild. The result was the extraordinary mock Tudor building we see today, but this is only visible in Great Marlborough Street. On the side of the store that faces Regent Street, Liberty had to stick to the Portland stone from which the rest of Regent Street is built, but in Great Marlborough Street he could do what he liked. And in the great tradition of craftsmanship and individuality championed by William Morris (1834–96), the man behind the Arts and Crafts movement, Liberty really let himself go in Great Marlborough Street.

Built around an interior courtyard, Liberty's conceals a remarkable and bizarre secret – it is made almost entirely from the magnificent oak timbers from two dismantled ships, HMS *Hindustan* and HMS *Impregnable*.

Not content with this, the owners of what was and still is one of London's most successful shops employed the best craftsmen – including several brought here specially from Italy – to install stained glass, magnificent staircases and superb carvings. Everything is handmade and unique.

What really ensured the success of Liberty's, however, was not the spectacular building, but the decision made much earlier by Gilbert and Sullivan to use Liberty fabrics for the costumes in their light opera *Patience* (1881).

Perhaps the most delightfully eccentric thing about Liberty's is that its staircases are built in such an odd way that at one time customers were always getting lost. All was resolved when, in the 1970s the then owners published a booklet which was available free to all regular customers entitled 'How Not to Get Lost in Liberty's'!

PENIS FOR SALE AT CHRISTIE'S
1972

When Napoleon Bonaparte died in May 1821 there were fears that rumours would spread about the manner of his death (recent claims include the suggestion that he was poisoned), which may explain why no fewer than 17 witnesses were invited to observe the autopsy which was carried out the day after he died by the Emperor's own doctor, Francesco Antommarchi.

On the Emperor's own instructions, his heart was removed first. Napoleon had asked that it be sent to his wife Marie-Louise, though the heart apparently vanished before it could be delivered.

The stomach was carefully examined and at the time it was agreed that cancer was the cause of death. Nothing else is recorded as having been removed. However within a few decades it was commonly supposed that Napoleon's penis had been cut off and stored away carefully during the autopsy. Oddly this was not mentioned by any of the 17 witnesses present at the time of the autopsy. But several commentators have suggested that the body was not guarded at all times during the procedure and while everyone's backs were turned Napoleon's organ could have been quickly snipped off.

Napoleon's friend Vignali, who administered the last rites, was left a large sum of money in Napoleon's will as well as numerous 'personal effects' – these were not specified.

Thirty years later Napoleon's manservant claimed that Vignali had indeed removed various parts of Napoleon's body, but this was not corroborated.

By 1916 the material bequeathed to Vignali had been sold *en masse* to a London collector, who some years later sold the collection on to an American. It was at this point that the penis story became more substantial. The description of the collection included the curious phrase mentioning 'the mummified tendon taken from Napoleon's body during the post-mortem'.

By the 1930s A.S. Rosenbach, an American collector, was displaying the 'tendon' in a blue velvet case and describing it as Napoleon's penis. It travelled to France and was later the centrepiece of a grand display at the Museum of French Art in New York.

A newspaper report described the organ as looking 'something like a maltreated strip of buckskin shoelace or shriveled eel'. Reports – largely stemming from Napoleon himself – that he was particularly well endowed seem to be contradicted by the fact that the organ was also described as 'one inch long and resembling a grape'.

The most extraordinary part of the story occurred in London in 1972 when the putative penis was put up for sale – complete with magnificent velvet-lined case – at the London auction house Christie's along with the rest of the Vignali collection. The collection failed to reach its reserve and was withdrawn. A few years later the penis popped up again, this time in Paris and unencumbered by all the other paraphernalia of the collection.

The penis was bought by John Lattimer, a retired professor of urology (appropriately enough) at the University of Columbia, for around $3,000. The penis is still, as it were, in Professor Lattimer's hands.

FAMILY MONEY ARRIVES
AFTER 200 YEARS

1976

Right across London ancient bequests are still being distributed to various good – and perhaps not so good – causes. Guy's Hospital enjoys the financial benefits of a number of bequests, some of which are centuries old. The British Library is another beneficiary of some odd legacies – it still receives upwards of half a million pounds a year as a result of a decision by George Bernard Shaw to leave his copyright fees to the British Museum Library (the predecessor of the British Library, which was established in 1973). He left the money, after his death in 1950, because as a penniless author back in the 1880s he had been able to work free of charge (and despite the holes in his shoes) every day in the warmth of the Museum's Reading Room with access to every book he needed.

The bizarre thing about that bequest is that it was not properly honoured. When the British Library separated from the British Museum something very odd and rather scandalous happened to Shaw's money. Museum officials are still cagey about the whole subject, but it looks as if Shaw's money goes to British Museum coffers rather than to the British Library, which of course goes entirely against Shaw's own wishes.

Other more ancient bequests are far more strictly administered, even when the amounts of money involved now seem tiny.

Among the most extraordinary ancient bequests was that made by a member of the Society of Antiquaries, whose base has been in Burlington House in Piccadilly for nearly 200 years. In 1776 the member left a considerable sum of money in a trust fund that benefited his family, but he stipulated that if his family should die out then the money should go to the Society of Antiquaries. In 1976 the last member of the family died and the money was duly paid over to the society, much to their astonishment.

TEARING UP £80,000
1979

Before he became rich and famous the painter Francis Bacon (1909–92) used to take his friends several times a week to Wheeler's Oyster Bar in Soho. He almost always insisted on paying despite having no regular income at all, which meant that he often had to ask the owner to allow him to run up a tab. Such was Bacon's astonishing charisma that the restaurant owner allowed the bill to reach more than £10,000 before he began to complain. Bacon had become quite well known by this time and the restaurant owner begrudgingly accepted a small Bacon painting as a sort of surety that the bill would eventually be paid. It was paid long before Bacon became a multimillionaire but the restaurateur kept the picture and eventually sold it for more than £250,000. A rare case of justified faith in an artist!

Bacon, a famous and outrageous habitué of Soho bars (most especially The Colony and the French House), was for decades at the centre of an outrageous clique of artists and writers around whom strange stories swirled like a dangerous mist. Among the most delightful is that he once spotted one of his own paintings in a shop in Bond Street and decided he didn't like it. He stepped into the shop, wrote a cheque for something in the region of £80,000, stepped back outside with the carefully wrapped picture under his arm and then smashed it to pieces, grinding the canvas underfoot until it was beyond the powers of any restorer to recover it.

HOW THE GOVERNMENT
LOST A HOSPITAL
1980

Foreigners always find the systems of land ownership and tenure in the UK completely baffling. The idea of leasehold, for example, is unknown in many countries, but in the UK it is combined with flying freeholds, tenants in common and a host of other bizarre methods of ownership.

In London until relatively recently titles that proved ownership of land were not registered – that meant that if you lost the paper that proved your ownership (your title) to land you also lost the land. These days land is registered with a government department so even if the title deeds are lost it is possible to look up the owner of a particular plot of land in official documents. But those buying leasehold property in London still frequently find that the freeholder has long vanished and they are advised by their lawyers that the freeholder may never be found – which produces the odd situation that a leaseholder can inherit a freehold at absolutely no cost.

One of the strangest tales of landownership in London concerns the famous St George's Hospital on London's Hyde Park Corner. The shell of the building remains to this day – the façade was preserved for a new hotel when the hospital finally closed in 1980 having been run continuously as a hospital since 1783.

When it closed, the government of the day looked forward to selling the land for development. They simply assumed that they owned the land as the hospital was by then part of the National Health Service and all hospital sites were government owned. As they prepared to sell the site – which was and is enormously valuable – they received a polite letter from the Duke of Westminster, whose family, the Grosvenors, own much of the land in Belgravia and Mayfair. The letter pointed out that the land on which the hospital was built was owned by the Grosvenors and not by the government. The government thought they were safe when they realised they had a 900-year lease on the ground, but again they were thwarted by the Grosvenor Estate, whose representatives had carefully kept the original deeds for more than two centuries.

The government certainly did own a very long lease on the land on which the hospital was built; that much was agreed, but when government officials were invited to take a careful look at the terms of the lease they discovered that it remained valid only if the land continued to be used for a hospital. Since a hospital was no longer required, the land reverted to the Grosvenors and the government was left with nothing.

ENDLESS SECRET TUNNELS

1980

When journalist Duncan Campbell found an entrance to a shaft in the middle of a traffic island in Bethnal Green in London's East End, he was astonished to discover a large tunnel at the bottom that led away into the distance apparently heading towards central London some 6 miles (9.7km) distant.

Campbell went home, collected his folding bike, and some time later returned to the shaft entrance. He carried the bike down the shaft and started pedalling towards central London along a series of extraordinary tunnels.

Over the centuries the curious have regularly come across underground tunnels beneath London's streets – some are ancient, others, as Campbell discovered, more modern. But the oddest thing is that there are almost certainly far more tunnels – many-layered and interconnecting – than we imagine.

Campbell's tunnel started about 100ft (30.5m) down and he rode around the tunnels for hours covering in excess of 12 miles (19.3km) in total, but it was clear to him, as it has been to others, that he had barely scratched the surface of London's extraordinary underground tunnel network.

Beautifully built brick-lined sewers, some dating back to medieval times, certainly exist in the oldest parts of the city and it is still possible to walk along the old bed of the Fleet River, which is now buried beneath Farringdon Street at the bottom of Ludgate Hill. The river – reduced to little more than a trickle – runs along the bottom of a giant pipe but there is plenty of room to walk.

In Victorian times the vast network of ancient sewers provided a living for hundreds of men and children – intimate knowledge of the tunnel routes was passed from one generation to the next and a team of sewer searchers might travel from the city to the West End and back in a day and always entirely underground, but they had to be careful: a sudden storm in Highgate or Hampstead could lead to flooding – a torrent of water hurtling along the tunnels would sweep the men to their deaths. Experienced sewer men knew the dangers and posted lookouts before they went down as well as trying to restrict their activities to days when the weather was fine. In the thick layers of human fat that lined the tunnels they would often find a rich store of lost gold trinkets and coins.

Those sewers are still there and beneath them, far deeper and almost as deep as London's water table, is a vast array of tunnels that some believe are part of a nuclear network of bunkers centred on Whitehall. There is some evidence for this too. We know, for example, that when the Jubilee line was built, planning permission for certain routes was refused, but officials would not say why. The same happens when telecommunications tunnels have to be dug – certain areas and depths and routes are always out of bounds because London under London is still the capital's greatest and most complex secret.

DARWIN ON THE UNDERGROUND

1985

Only the very superstitious – meaning the religious – now seriously question the validity of Darwin's theory of evolution. Darwin's idea about the survival of the fittest has been widely misinterpreted it is true – by 'fittest' Darwin meant best adapted for survival in a particular environment, not strongest or toughest. Darwin also explained that time was the great factor in evolution: when groups of individuals of the same species are separated by some physical barrier – say a mountain range or an ocean – for long enough they will gradually change to such an extent that they would no longer be able to breed if they were brought together again. They would, in short, have become two different species.

Astonishingly, London's Underground provides a splendid example of Darwinism in action. In the mid-1980s scientists noticed that as well as the numerous rats and mice living in the Victorian tunnels deep under the streets of the capital there were also large numbers of mosquitoes.

Nothing particularly unusual about that, except that studies quickly revealed that the mosquitoes were very different from other known mosquitoes. Comparisons were made with similar insects from Africa and Asia and with all the known subspecies of mosquito and the London mosquito was sufficiently different to be labelled a new species.

How on earth could this happen? The answer is evolution by natural selection but in a speeded-up form.

Scientists pieced together the likely history of the London mosquito.

When the tunnels of the Underground were first being built at the end of the nineteenth century mosquitoes would have been more common than they are now, although they are still common enough. The pools of stagnant water inevitable in and around building sites would have provided perfect breeding grounds for the insects and when the tunnels were finally closed in the mosquitoes found themselves underground. As the years passed they reproduced and gradually migrated all along the system wherever there was water. Today mosquitoes exist in the deepest parts of the system and tests have shown that they can no longer interbreed with any other known species of mosquito – physical isolation has made them change to the point where they have become a separate species, exactly as Darwin predicted.

The reason they have changed in a relatively short time is that a century is not in fact a short time at all when seen in relation to the lifespan of a mosquito. Those tunnel mosquitoes have probably gone through thousands of generations in the time they have been isolated.

LOST LAVATORIES

1985

One of the great tragedies of the past 50 years is the gradual disappearance of London's magnificent public lavatories. Built into the fabric of the environment by nineteenth-century urban planners who were concerned (unlike modern developers) that their buildings should be decorative as well as functional, public lavatories tended to be built at major street junctions and below ground.

But, much as the Victorian pub builder wanted to celebrate his skill in the sumptuousness of gin palaces with their sparkling cut glass, fabulous mirrors and huge ornate ceilings and walls, so the lavatory builders created splendid subterranean palaces of gleaming copper pipework, hugely decorative tiles and basins, and lavatories with delicate flower decoration. Heavy mahogany doors were used for each lavatory cubicle and the overall impression was always one of spacious loftiness, for these were palaces to ease and bodily contentment.

As it cost a penny to use these grand public conveniences the Victorian lavatory also gave us the splendid euphemism that survives to this day: the phrase 'I'm going to spend a penny' being among the politest and most delicate indications that one wishes to use the loo.

The grand Victorian lavatories were gradually taken out of use by penny-pinching local authorities who simply assumed that the growth in cafés and restaurants would fill the gap – if the modern city dweller needs to spend a penny she has to go into an expensive restaurant for a cup of coffee she may well not want simply to use the loo.

But oddly, though many of the old public loos were closed and their entrances sealed over, many still exist complete with all their magnificent pipework below ground, buried like Egyptian tombs and awaiting some enthusiastic future lavatorial archaeologist.

One of the last lavatories to go was the splendid example in Covent Garden just outside the church in the piazza. Here in its dying days in the 1980s you could spend a penny and listen to opera, for the lavatory attendant was a keen opera buff who also decorated the walls with reproductions of some of the National Gallery's most famous pictures. Tourists and Londoners flocked to this eccentric destination, and rightly so, until it was closed by unimaginative local officials.

Odder still than the Covent Garden lavatory was the public loo that once stood in the middle of the road about halfway along High Holborn. So magnificent were the fittings in this the ultimate public lavatory that they are now in the Victoria and Albert Museum, a testament to the public-spiritedness and architectural pride of our Victorian ancestors.

The brass and mahogany fittings of the Holborn public loo were surmounted by a set of superb cut-glass cisterns. These were spectacular enough to provoke comment in numerous newspapers but the enthusiasm of the public for them knew no bounds when an attendant in the 1930s decided that each cistern would be far more interesting stocked with goldfish. He duly stocked them and the fish lived happily in the sparkling clean water to the delight of patrons for many years – until in fact the Holborn public loo suffered the fate of almost every other public loo in London.

HOW CRIME BECAME ART

1995

In 1962 the future playwright Joe Orton, whose plays
Loot and *Entertaining Mr Sloane* were later to astonish
theatregoers, was arrested along with his lover for defacing
library books.

Contrast that with the last year of Orton's extraordinary
– and sadly rather short – life. The year 1967 saw the first
performance of his play *What the Butler Saw,* the latest
in a string of theatrical successes. But Kenneth Halliwell,
Orton's lover since 1951, found it difficult to cope with his
partner's increasing fame and in a fit of depression killed
Orton with a hammer while he slept and then took a massive
overdose of sleeping pills.

The newspaper obituaries tended to dwell on what was
then described as Orton's 'unnatural relationship' with
Halliwell and his outrageous behaviour.

The incident of the 1962 book-defacing offence was also
dredged up. After the court trial of 1962 both Orton and
Halliwell had been sentenced to six months' imprisonment
but the public was outraged – not by the severity of the
sentence, but by its lenity.

One commentator said: 'People who deface library
books must be dead to all sense of shame; six months'
imprisonment, the severest sentence that the law allowed,
is totally inadequate for a crime of that kind.'

Yet how strange is the world that over 30 years later Islington Library – the very library that instituted the prosecution against Orton and Halliwell – could proudly proclaim that an exhibition of the books defaced was to be held. Anyone wanting to visit the exhibition and see the images that outraged an earlier generation now had to pay an entrance fee. The defaced books – showing among other things Winston Churchill's head on an ape – had become enormously valuable and still are. They are now among the library's most prized possessions. If Orton had never become famous the books no doubt would have been thrown away long ago – such is the extraordinary power of celebrity.

ANIMALS AT WAR

2004

A monument unveiled in London's Park Lane in 2004 is the first ever to recognise the enormous contribution various animals made to Britain's efforts during the First and Second World Wars.

The monument shows a horse, a dog, two mules and a sad list of the number of animals killed as a result of human aggression, but what makes the monument so extraordinary is the range of animals it commemorates – apart from horses, dogs and mules there are pigeons and even glow worms.

One historian has said that it was the British love of animals and their inventive relationships with them that made key differences at crucial times to the ability of British forces to win campaign after campaign. Some of the assistance given by animals is so strange as to be almost unbelievable – glow worms for example really were used in the Great War to enable soldiers to read their maps at night!

The most fascinating part of this strange monument, however, is the detailed list of some 60 animals each awarded the Dickin Medal since 1943. The Dickin is the animal equivalent of The Victoria Cross medal given for conspicuous gallantry.

Among the 62 recipients of the Dickin Medal there are 32 pigeons, 18 dogs, three horses and a cat – all from the Second World War.

All the stories of these animals are remarkable. Take Winkie the pigeon who flew more than 100 miles (160km) with her wings badly clogged with oil in order to save a bomber crew that had ditched in the sea; or Rob, a dog in the parachute regiment, who made more than 20 parachute jumps into Africa on dangerous missions with the Special Armed Services.

Then during the recent war in Iraq there was Buster, a springer spaniel who detected a huge cache of arms saving the lives of many civilians and soldiers; mine detector dog Ricky carried on working after receiving head injuries from an explosion.

During the Blitz in London, dogs such as Beauty, Peter, Irma and Jet, located survivors buried in buildings destroyed by the Germans' nightly bombing raids.

The inscription on the monument in Park Lane reads: 'Animals in War. This monument is dedicated to all the animals that served and died alongside British and Allied forces in wars and campaigns throughout time. They had no choice.'

DEATH BY PELICAN

2006

There have been pelicans on the lake at St James's Park since the first few were presented to Charles II by the Czar of Russia in 1660. Nothing so exotic had ever been seen in the capital and Londoners flocked to the park to see the new arrivals.

By the early 1970s disease and bad luck had reduced the St James's flock of pelicans to just one bird. Something had to be done and with a sense of tradition typical of the Court of St James, it was recalled that the original birds had been presented by the Imperial Russian Court.

Despite the Cold War the British Government approached the Russian Government and asked if they could spare a few more birds. When the birds arrived everyone was delighted – except the other birds in the park.

The newspapers were filled with stories of songbirds and more especially pigeons being eaten by the pelicans – the stories were not generally believed because pelicans are not carnivores, but the experts had not reckoned on these new and very ferocious Communist pelicans. Proof was difficult to obtain until in 2006 a photographer managed to get a close-up picture of a plump woodpigeon disappearing into a pelican's gaping maw!

GOING DUTCH

2007

Dutch ships that land their cargoes in the City of London –
admittedly a rare event today when most cargo is unloaded
miles downriver at Tilbury – are never charged harbour
fees.

In fact they have paid no fees since the plague year
of 1665 when London was virtually cut off from the rest of
the world.

No other nation would land its cargoes at that time for fear
of catching the terrible disease; only the Dutch kept trading
with London, dropping supplies of food and other goods
vital to the survival of a city which has shown its gratitude
ever since by waiving the charges that apply to all other
nations.

OTHER TITLES IN

THE STRANGEST SERIES

The *Strangest* series has been delighting and enthralling readers for decades with weird, exotic, spooky and baffling tales of the absurd, ridiculous and the bizarre. This range of fascinating books – from Football to London, Rugby to Law and many subjects in between – details the very curious history of each one's funniest, oddest and most compelling characters, locations and events.

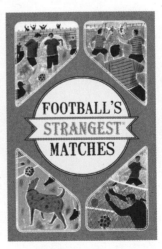

9781910232910

9781910232866

9781910232934

9781910232972

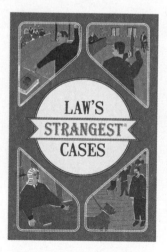

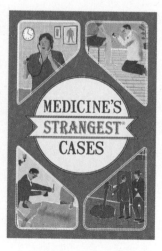

9781910232897

9781910232941

254

9781910232965

9781910232873

9781910232927

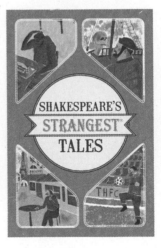

9781910232903

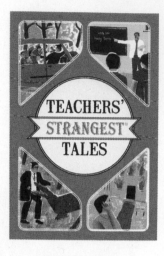

9781910232989

9781910232958